T0066905

BOOKS BY THE SAME AUTHOR

1. Scattered Matherticles: Mathematical Reflections, Volume I (2010)
2. Vectors in History: Main Foci - India and USA, Volume I (2012)
3. Epsilons of Deltas of Life: Everyday Stories, Volume I (2012)
4. My Hindu Faith & Periscope, Volume I (2012)
5. Via Bhatinda: A Braid of Reflected Memoirs, Volume I (2013)
6. Swami Deekshanand Saraswati: My Swami Mama Ji Volume I (2014)
7. Darts on History of Mathematics Volume I (2014)

Converging Mantherticles:

Mathematical Reflections

Volume II

Satish C. Bhatnagar

Order this book online at www.trafford.com
or email orders@trafford.com

Most Trafford titles are also available at major online book retailers.

© Copyright 2015 Satish C. Bhatnagar.
All rights reserved. No part of this publication may be reproduced, stored in a retrieval
system, or transmitted, in any form or by any means, electronic, mechanical, photocopying,
recording, or otherwise, without the written prior permission of the author.

Print information available on the last page.

ISBN: 978-1-4907-5730-8 (sc)
ISBN: 978-1-4907-5731-5 (e)

Because of the dynamic nature of the Internet, any web addresses or links contained in
this book may have changed since publication and may no longer be valid. The views
expressed in this work are solely those of the author and do not necessarily reflect the
views of the publisher, and the publisher hereby disclaims any responsibility for them.

Any people depicted in stock imagery provided by Thinkstock are models,
and such images are being used for illustrative purposes only.
Certain stock imagery © Thinkstock.

Trafford rev. 05/01/2015

Trafford
PUBLISHING   www.trafford.com

North America & international
toll-free: 1 888 232 4444 (USA & Canada)
fax: 812 355 4082

DISTRIBUTION OF CONTENTS

II.   CONTEMPARAY SCENARIOS

EXCERPTS FROM THE READERS

Satish, I really agree with your observations. Your point of view is further reinforced by an opinion piece in the Sunday, April 1 RJ written by a Western High School math teacher by the name of Barone, if I remember correctly…. Dave Emerson **(# 03)** Emeritus Dean of College of Sciences

Why should we consider calculus or mathematics particularly suited to teaching ethics? During teaching I have indeed found that I make remarks on ethics. But I have considered it as part of my rambling. It won't appear on the test!! Personally, I consider it very valuable because the students are going to, in their later lives, forget differentiation anyway. Regards. Shankar RAJA (# 04), Emeritus Physics Professor

Very enjoyable! I was informed of some research on math performance--where those taking an exam did significantly better when starting with easy and proceeding to hard (as compared to hard, then easy). I think building confidence (without sacrificing content and academic rigour) is important and easier said than done! Good idea with how you started the course. Aaron Harris (# 24) Doctoral student, Math Edu.

Good points, Satish. If I had my way, the high schools would not be allowed to teach calculus. Too many of my Honors Calculus I classes were spoiled by those kids who took calculus in high school and learned nothing more than the tricks and short cuts. They make the kids who did not take high school calculus believe that these other kids were smarter because they know the tricks. Give me kids who took solid geometry and analytic geometry in high school because they will be ready for calculus. Paul Aizley Emeritus UNLV math professor and three-term Nevada Assemblyman (#34)

I always like your notes. Hope you are having a great time! Even as we turn our gaze inward, our future lies in looking out as you have noted. Best wishes

Neal Smatresk, Former Provost and President at UNLV, and now President of North Texas University since 2014 (#44).

Satish Dear- Beautiful - very original. I wish you were teaching when I was doing MA. Actually, even myself - I wish I could be doing Math MA now at this maturity and understanding when I can comprehend almost anything that is written. Subhash Puri, Motivational speaker and author (#50)

Hi Satish: I have enjoyed reading this eye-opener 'reflection.' The 'infinity' you have postulated has that undefinable 'infinity' of Hinduism which explains the 'infinity' of gods and goddesses in the Hindu pantheon--the Hindu minds are open and not constricted by excessive number of prayers and finite scriptures and treatises. Satyan Moorty, Emeritus Professor of English, Southern University (#54)

Satish, Thank you for this. I appreciate both the wisdom and wit (Viagra and testosterone) in this reflection. Many thanks for sharing with me and sincere wishes of good luck in your pursuit of this award. Best wishes, Richard Schori (#70) Emeritus Professor, University of Oregon

DEDICATED

TO

"MATHEMATICAL THINKING"

EXCERPTS FROM THE PREFACE OF VOLUME I

Background

Lately, I have not started on a book or adopted a mathematics textbook without reading author's preface, introduction, or foreword. It aptly applies to my collection of *Reflections* too. Now, I asked these questions from myself: What good these *Mathematical Reflections* are? Who are going to enjoy reading, or benefit from them? What is my claim to their worth? It took me nearly four years to go for publication. These *Reflections* are a good reading for general public curious about mathematical tidbits, and for mathematics students and faculty especially from India and the US. They have curricular issues, histories, cross-cultural perspectives, and typical faculty and student scenarios extracted from classrooms, professional meetings, conventions, and the department hallways. ....

How did the *Reflections* start?

'Serious' writing has been in my nature for many years. In a nutshell, these *Reflections* are re-incarnations of the old-fashioned letters that I loved to write, receive, read, and collect since my 20s. Seven years ago, after having written several *Reflections*, I looked back at them for a possible categorization. It then became essential to separate out the *Mathematical Reflections*. Also, there is something technical and alarming about mathematics in the minds of the laypersons. ....

Two Words on my English

This *reflective* preface won't be complete without it. I went to high school and college in Bathinda, the hinterland of Punjab. I was a rebel when it came to learning grammar and spellings. For instance, I spelled 'miltary' for 'military' for years, and got penalized. In fairness, neither the punctuation was taught well, nor was I receptive to it. For years, I have believed that the contents should prevail over the dressing of the grammar. Punctuation, like black pepper, should be sprinkled over a dish for its flavor, not for the taste.

Well, once I started having ambitions of becoming a non-fiction writer of some stature, I eventually realized the importance of grammar and punctuation. At least, clear sense and meanings in writings must be conveyed to the readers. In addition to these pronouncements, I enjoy coining new expressions and words, like '*matherticles*' in the title of this volume, derived from 'mathematics' and 'particles'. Minor grammatical rules are flouted here and there, particularly in the usages of the article, 'the', commas (,) and semi colons (;) and space (-).

However, there is a real story about my English accent and comprehension. Forty-two years ago, when I first faced the accent issue in the US, I fought it long to retain my North Indian enunciation. Coming to the US at age 29, my vocal cords and guttural muscles were set in place. Mathematics being a 'language', I focused on it for my doctorate too. Now I teasingly tell my students, "You are learning from me an English accent, which is free of cost in addition to mathematics that you pay for. Moreover, nearly 300 million people in North Indian subcontinent speak with my accent." As far as comprehension is concerned, Indiana University Mathematics Department had laid out a policy that for Indian students, English was not their foreign language, as they were better at it than the Americans - particularly when it came to reading and writing. Therefore, in order to satisfy the two-foreign language requirement for Math PhD, I had to choose the two out of French, German and Russian.

Indians have been producing great literary works in English for the last 100 years, but they are not recognized in academic circles, or for international awards, simply because their literary style is different from the British and American norms. That has bothered me for years. Now that I am 70, I can confidently say that my writing style neither falls under standard English of the US, nor of contemporary India. It is uniquely Indo-USA in usage, imagery, structure and phrases. It is integral to my being, and hence carries a distinct stamp on my writings.......

Writing has offered me a glimpse into *Self-Realization*. After a while, you have to let the contents prevail. In life, you can't to be too protective of your nascent ideas, as we are towards our children. Both have to face the scrutiny of the world outside. Hence, it is time to look forward to the next phase of how these *Reflections* fare, or how well prepared they went out.

Satish C. Bhatnagar

Sep 12, 2010

A CONVERGING PREFACE

Writing the preface of a book is the crowning moment of its completion. Sometimes, I start working on it, as thoughts and ideas are springing up in my mind, but on a few occasions, it could be the last item of the book. It reminds me of a 'topping off' ceremony, when the topmost storey is reached in the construction of high-rise towers, having 80+ levels. After a celebration by the ironworkers, the construction cranes on the top are dis-assembled – an engineering feat in itself.

For two solid months, I went through every line of the manuscript – revising, editing, polishing and tinkering with the text here and there. There is no exaggeration in saying that each reflection goes through at least ten major or minor revisions before its inclusion in a book. Strangely enough, with each publication of a book, I am progressively becoming 'possessive' of my writing style – both in its syntax and semantics. This time, I felt a certain degree of 'sacredness' about it to the extent that I dispelled any thoughts of having it edited by an outsider. A gut feeling arose - that anybody else doing the final editing would 'defile' my work. Before submitting it to the publishers, the last farewell touches have to be mine!

This is the second volume of mathematical reflections. The first volume, published in 2010, had ninety-seven reflections written during 1988-2006. The reason it did not have a nice round number like 100 was that I chose the cutoff point as the calendar year 2006. This time, I preferred an even number of 70 (how it became 73 is another story). They cover a period of 2007 to 2012, though six of them still go back to 1991-2004. The reason for their exclusion in Volume I is simple. They were saved in the Word files, but from their names, I had no idea of their contents! Yes, I had given the names to those files, but my forgetfulness of certain routine things alone complements my brand of originality.

The title of the first volume is ***Scattered Matherticles*** – 'Scattered', because I had no vision of their individual or collective placements when I started writing in 2000. Sending reflections for publication in the journals has never fitted my mind-set. My books alone show them in print first. The first volume just evolved by itself, but it laid out a path for the second volume, which is rightly called *Converging Matherticles*.

What is innovative about this book? I am always cognizant about it, as I do not want to add to any pollution - particularly to the print pollution, not even in the name of research and scholarly activities. Professionally, I am far beyond academic tenure and promotion considerations, where any publication counts. The books are essentially open sources in both the print and electronic media.

Above all, my format of reflections, which are independent, personable, and identifiable, remains unique. They are only turned out when I am turned on to something. It is seldom done for the sake of writing a piece. Amazingly, at this stage, I capture only one-third of them in writing. With this outlook, I am confident that everyone will find a few pieces enjoyable to their taste.

How is Volume II different from Volume I? The organization of the material is slightly different – having grown out of experience. In Volume I, all the 97 reflections were in one block and arranged chronologically. Volume I was my first baby ever in the publishing venture. I have wised up a bit since then, when it comes to the layouts of a book. In Volume II, all the 73 reflections are loosely divided into three sections; nevertheless, the time line is preserved in each section. Yes, I believe that the date and place of a reflection provide a better perspective with which a reader can deeply relate to.

At the time of the writing of Volume I, the selective comments of my non-traditional readers were not even thought of. After including them in other books, a few comments of selected readers are included in Volume II. As a corollary, there are spaces for Personal Remarks too. I like this feature, as I always need them for brief notes made inside the book that I read. Also, thumbnail sketches of the main commenters are given at the end –but, no index or a bibliography.

What is the content distribution? Thirty-nine reflections in Section I are all drawn from the classroom settings. However, some of them fly off - like, connecting a proof in mathematics to the choreography of a dance, and so on. Its title, **TEACHING PRISM**, is therefore justifiable. It also includes a few reflections from my teaching in Spring-2009 at the University of Nizwa in the Sultanate of Oman.

Section II is called, **CONTEMPORARY SCENARIOS.** It contains fifteen reflections including a few that were written in Oman. They largely focus on individuals, like one connecting with the founding father, Benjamin Franklin. Section III is titled as - **ASSORTMENT OF REFLECTIONS.** It has nineteen reflections on challenging topics – like, mathematization of religion and life forces. Some of them could not be completed on account of their challenging nature. I hope someone will take each one up, where I have left it off, say, at a point P, and carry it through the point Z. In addition, a few reflections are drawn from the mathematics conferences that I regularly attend in the US and overseas.

Dedication The Volume I was not dedicated to any person, so does it stay for Volume II. However, I am increasingly getting convinced of the power of mathematical thinking. Its essence is deductive reasoning. In my lectures, I bring out its contrast with the thought processes needed in the sciences, law, poetry, politics, and so on. Therefore, Volume II is firmly dedicated to 'Mathematical Thinking', a major window of my life!

Thank-You Time: Anjali, my 26-year old granddaughter, always assists me in all sundry glitches – both technical and non-technical. She just earned a doctorate in Occupational Therapy from Washington University, St Louis. Francis A. Andrew has provided valuable feedback to each and every reflection since we became friends in Nizwa, Oman. He has been teaching English in the Middle East for nearly thirty-four years. In a subtle way, he has re-kindled my love for the English language at my age of 75. Love does not come easy for anything during this phase of life!

Any comments and suggestions on the book are welcome, and they would be thankfully acknowledged. Use the e-mail ID: viabti1968@ gmail.com for communication. The Journey goes on!

Satish C. Bhatnagar

March 06, 2015

GLOSSARY AND ABBREVIATONS

Advaitya; non-duality - Principle of one-ness.

Guru is far more than a high school and college instructor. There is an associated element of one-one-ness between a teacher and disciple, loftiness and holistic nature - bordering spirituality.

Gurukul is a kind of Hindu seminary school going back to the Vedic period in India.

Kundalini is a state of enlightenment achieved in a path of self-realization.

Mantra is set of supposedly energized syllables in Sanskrit – potent enough to affect material changes with right repetition and enunciation.

*Rish*i is an enlightened individual in terms of his/her cultivated powers of mind developed through Yoga over a long period of time.

Shrimad Bhaagvatam or Bhagvat is a holy scripture of the Hindus. It is often confused with Gita or Bhagvat Gita, which is a central part of a chapter in the epic of Mahabharata. Whereas, Shrimad Bhagvat was compiled by Vyas after he had finished the Mahabharata. It is a great story of life.

Siddhis are the states of mind achieved after years of penance and yoga that one can even materialize objects. Essentially, it is a reverse mass-energy equation. The late Satya Sai Baba of Puttapurthy had reputation to pull out of thin air jewelry items for his followers all over the world. Such a person is called *Siddha*

Sutra is a cryptic and condensed description of a principle or property. An example is of 18 *sutras* of Vedic Mathematics.

Upvedas and *Vedangas* are ancillary treatises for a systematic study of the Vedas.

Tapa is combination of penance, meditation with austerities.

Vedas refer to the most ancient four Hindu scriptures, namely; *Rig, Yajur, Atharva, and Saam.*

Yog/Yoga means a union with the Supreme - for which the body is prepared with *aasans* (specific physical postures) and *pranayama* (specific breathing exercises) for holding energy of the life force drawn with concentration of mind and meditation on the Supreme, which is a Limit of all human potentialities.

IT: Information Technology
BTI: Bhatinda or Bathinda
DLH: for Delhi, the capital of India
UNLV: University of Nevada Las Vegas
JMM: Joint Mathematics Meetings
MAA: Mathematical Association of America
AMS: American Mathematical Society
NAM: National Association of Mathematicians (Founded by
　　Afro-Americans)
AWM: Association of Women in Mathematics
SIAM: Society of Industrial and Applied Mathematics
IMS: Indian Mathematical Society
Math: Popular abbreviation for Mathematics - used interchangeably in the book
PDE: Partial Differential Equation(s)
ODE: Ordinary Differential Equation(s)

CAPTURING CONVERGENCE

The front cover of a book must reveal a bit about the contents of the book too. It is in the spirit of a principle of truth-in-lending. However, that is not the case often. In modern marketing, sex sells and sex stops a person in the tracks. However, the effect of sex is orgasmic - lasting for a short time. I am not a professional in the writing commercial ads. Also, I am not an artist by training, though I regularly visit art galleries. Nevertheless, I am getting deeper into the designing of the front covers of my own books.

The main challenge is to capture both the contents and the title of the book, *CONVERGING MATHERTICLES: MATHEMATICAL REFLECTIONS, VOLUME II.* For the last ten years, making connections between two remote concepts, ideas, and objects has been engaging my mind so much so that I encourage my students in this type of thinking too. For extra credits, many students have connected concepts and techniques in a math course with whatever they are passionate about - be it another math course, hobby, or job. That has resulted in a collection of very readable pieces worthy of a compilation in a student book of its own kind.

Seven years ago, I coined this word, 'matherticle', when I finished my first book. It stems from two words, 'mathematical' and 'particle'. I have been enamored of tiny subatomic particles in mathematical physics for their elusive beauty. My mathematical reflections do have beauty and mystery – though drawn from simple scenarios. That is how I see a connection between matherticles and mathematical reflections.

The next question concerns their images. Well, I go to mathematical symbols, which are the nuts & bolts and nails & screws of mathematics. The letters of the Greek and Roman alphabets are the most popular ones in mathematical sciences. While teaching, I always toss in some characters from the Hindi, Punjabi, and Urdu alphabets that I also know. Since each reflection crisscrosses and ricochets from 2-3 nodal points, I want these symbols like a dozen kinds of beans in a soup. Having a formula or equation on the cover may send a wrong message on the contents, as it is not a book of mathematics. It is meant for students and people, who are curious about the entire mathematical culture. In teaching too, I do not talk over the heads of the students. Keeping math simple is not the same as trivializing it or diluting it.

Now, the question is about how to capture the convergence. Visually, spirals are the best. I want to see all the symbols in different colors. The Greek alphabet is in white, English in red, Hindi in saffron yellow, Urdu in dark green, and Punjabi in bright blue. The background color of the front and back cover is a shade of blue, which should be a notch darker than the blue color used in Volume I.

The spiral is the heart of the cover for making a visual effect. The symbols, which are farther from the 'eye' of the cyclone, may look gone astray - making no pattern. However, as they get closer to the 'center', a pattern should begin to form. That is likely to capture good convergence.

Trafford's design department seems to have good artists. They are able to read off my mind from such a note and transform it into a picture that I do end up liking. Many readers have complimented me on the front covers of my books. For the record, my son and granddaughter had put the first cover together. Reason: I thought this task was just beyond my mathematical mind – forgetting the worldwide fusion going on between art and mathematics. I look forward to seeing the first proof of the cover. It usually takes 2-3 iterations before it is finalized.

March 06, 2015

SECTION I

TEACHING PRISM

HONORED IN HONORING

[**Note**: For a number of reasons, I debated about including this write-up as the opening piece of this volume, but my adherence on the chorology of my reflections prevailed ultimately.

Friday, April 30 was the day to recognize the distinguished faculty and students in the College of Sciences at UNLV for the academic year 2003-04. In the past, there used to separate functions for the students and faculty. This one was better organized and attended. Being myself the 2004-winner of the College Distinguished Service Award, it made a bit special for me. In addition, as the Associate Dean of the College, I gave the closing remarks at the function whereas; Dean Yasbin had given the opening remarks.

I take this opportunity of updating on the Bhatnagar Awards established in 2002 through an endowment fund with the UNLV Foundation. They are not one-time awards, but annual for perpetuity. At present, two Bhatnagar Awards are given out in cash: $600 to the Top Major in mathematics and $300 to the Top Minor in mathematics. It may be worth pointing out that the number of awards for the students in biology, chemistry and geosciences run in 20 -30, but in mathematics, Bhatnagar Awards are the only two awards! **No matter how valuable mathematics is lauded publicly, there are relatively few donors who would promote mathematics.** That was one of the reasons to establish these awards.

However, the vision in the Memorandum of Understanding includes awards in English and Education in near future. I invite everyone to become a partner and contributor to the Fund. You can do it online, or send your contributions directly to the UNLV Foundation. Go to www.unlv.edu. Click on the "Donate Online" field. **Account name** is Bhatnagar Awards and **Account number** is 330779. Or, directly send a cheque to the UNLV Foundation (**Mark the check for the Bhatnagar Awards**) 4505 Maryland Parkway South, Box 451006, Las Vegas, NV 89154-1006.

Let me also add, that many US institutions match contributions to universities. So do check it with the Human Resources Department. Of course, all contributions are tax deductibles. To make it memorable, you may like to associate your donation with a birthday, anniversary, graduation, promotion, wedding, or any celebration of life, at any time during the year.

The following are the winners of the Bhatnagar Awards:

	TOP Major	TOP Minor
2003	Patrick Bennett	Tundra De
2004	Daniel Corral and Adam Winchester (**Tied**)	Edwin So

May 03, 2004

PS: As of 01/2015, the Bhatnagar Award remains the sole annual awards at UNLV in mathematics. Out of these three math major winners, two have completed PhDs in mathematics and Daniel's is delayed due to his changing the graduate school twice. Tondra De got PhD in Science Education from UCLA. The top mathematics students have been identified through the year 2015, but their names are included elsewhere.]

COMMENTS

Dear Dr. Bhatnagar: Thanks for this letter and it is very wonderful thing you have established and I will work on it and check my company Bechtel foundation for matching. We are very proud of you for the thing you do for every one. Regards, **Venkatrao Thummala**

MY 'SENIOR' STUDENTS

"How are you, Lloyd? I am Satish Bhatnagar." "I appreciate your calling," he softly responded. Lloyd is a 70+ year old student in my course, *History of Mathematics* (MAT 714). On the first day of class introduction, all my students fill out an 8-point student profile. One of the items is: **What are your expectations in this course?** The range of responses that the students have given over the years can be put together into a little storybook.

However, Lloyd wrote only one word, **Enlightenment**. To which I remarked, "You are in the right place and hopefully with a right instructor!" After all, who spend more of their lime seeking spiritual enlightenment than the Hindus? Self-Realization, Law of Karma, salvation, enlightenment etc. have been the staple foods for their intellect for millennia.

Lloyd is not the first septuagenarian student in the classes. Such students are very common at UNLV. On my very first day of teaching in Aug 1974, Leo Schuman was in my Differential Equations Course. He was 68 and I was then 34. On getting sick of puttering around the house for a year after retirement, Leo decided to go for MS in mathematics. His wife was also happy to see him leave home. He turned out to be one of the best students. After MS, he taught in the Department as a part-time instructor for ten years. Around the same time, Art was another 80+ year old student, who took only math graduate courses "to keep the sanity of mind". He was not interested in getting any degree. The presence of such 'senior' students in the class pushes the young ones to excel, and keeps the instructors on their toes.

The number of students over 65 took a quantum leap 20 years ago when UNLV instituted a policy of not charging any fees from them. It is common in most US institutions. **This defines western culture, or more specifically, the American culture**. The social institutions in India are so much structured that it is unthinkable for any one after 50 to attend college for keeping the mind engaged. My mother always bemoaned at my studying after PhD. It took my wife several years to understand the American love for life-long learning.

Lloyd had his MS & PhD (1962) in statistics from Columbia University. He comes from an era when statistics was not duly respected in traditional mathematics departments. It reminds me of the state of mathematics education presently. In another context, Lloyd told me of his taking calculus courses from Peter Lax, now one of the famous mathematicians, and 2005-winner of the Abel Prize recently instituted in 2003. Since he had witnessed events that are considered history for the younger generation, I have assigned him a project on the history of lower division statistics courses since 1957.

While turning in his first weekly report, Lloyd told me of his having to miss classes for the next 2-3 weeks because of a major surgery. He was matter-of-fact about it, and I wished him well. His report has a unique touch about it that ended as: "This first week of the course has been very productive for me. If the remaining weeks are equally so, I don't know how I will find time to do everything." Nevertheless, this little note made my day!

Feb 02, 2007/Mar 2010

COMMENTS

It is motivating to me do MS in Math and do some teaching after retirement. **Hardev Singh**

That was an interesting piece. **Abraham**

ALL ABOUT EXAMPLES!

March is a pollen-laden allergy month in Las Vegas, but as a mathematics instructor, round the year, I remain 'allergic' to the examples in the textbooks! I seldom work them in my classes, as I consider it no teaching. The textbook examples are for the students to self-study the material before its class presentation, and work them out independently. Last week, a scenario burst opened my entire stand on it. Actually, my stance on examples varies with the level of a course. Generally, I tell my students, **"Take examples and worked out problems, as intellectual challenge in figuring them out!"** Growing number of hint(s) to the routine exercises, is another story. After all, life is about tackling new situations.

There is a saga behind examples. During my four years (1955-59) in a Bathinda College (India), I had a score of math courses taken from only two instructors. One would routinely come a few minutes late, open the textbook, literally copy down a couple of examples on the black board with his back towards the students, and walk out before the period was over. Such instructors are lazy, incompetent and unprofessional.

As a student, I never envisioned a career in college teaching then. But after starting full time college teaching 'accidentally' in 1961, I decided never to spend class time on the examples! Ironically, the vacancy was caused by the same 'lazy' instructor going on extended leave to serve in the Indian Army! Since then, so much water has gone underneath my math bridge professionally. I have taught in six different cultures and foreign countries. Students are unique in each institution. But nowhere, the culture of a city influences the students as observed at UNLV. It takes new faculty several years to realize it.

The amazing thing about UNLV students is the change that they subtly bring out in the instructors. It is geologic, but quite revealing. This year, I am teaching an upper division 2-semeser sequence on Ordinary Differential Equations (ODE), (MATH 427-428). I have already done it six times, and the last round was 15 years ago. The archive of my test problems clearly tells the tale of my 'lowered expectations'. Yet, my present students consider me as their toughest instructor!

A few years ago, I decided to include at least one example on a class test. **The main objective is to impress upon the students the unique nature of mathematics.** One can't claim full understanding of a problem by simply reading it or watching someone do it. Present students are becoming increasingly visual learners, but visual learning never applies to math problems, no matter how small the parts are. Each step has to be worked out and connected for a complete solution of a problem. The number of students getting the examples right on tests and quizzes has been steadily decreasing. And, it is happening coast to coast. A friend in the University of Delaware shared similar stories.

A week before the 2nd class test, I quizzed on an example appearing in 2-3 different contexts. Only one, out of 14, got it right! As the quiz was returned at the following meeting, a chorus of students wanted the quiz problem discussed. They did not care to figure it out even after the quiz! Two days later, they were staring at it in the class. I had planned to do some reviewing, touch-up on some material, and give a few test tips. If I adhere to my principle of not discussing this example, then some students may be psychologically affected. A good state of mind is no less important than preparation for a test. So 'quietly' I worked out that example. But they wanted to see more details behind each detail! Nearly 25 minutes were gone into that example, yet one student wanted to 'see' more, as if he was watching a strip-tease dancer!

It turned into my *Reflection*: where is mathematics heading to at UNLV? Based upon the courses that I have taught, the undergraduates at UNLV don't care about dropping courses and re-taking them till they pass it to their expectations. It makes sense when their priority is job over the courses of studies. It is paramount to teach at UNLV with this reality check. Nationally, I am not pessimistic about the US undergraduates in math. **As long as the types of the undergraduates honored at the Joint Mathematics Meetings continue to be attracted towards mathematics - its future is safe for a while.**

Another reality is that the present students have more course delivery options than available before. Inversely, their attitude towards joy and challenge in learning math is narrowing like their attention study span. Being a student of history, the rise and fall of civilizations is my perennial topic of study and contemplation. As long as the immigrants continue to provide cheap manual labor needed in the US farms and factories, and foreign students replenish the intellectual forces in researches, the US economy would continue to roll. But once the inflow slows down and the national economies reverse, the US would face its 'historic' decline in the fall of nations and civilizations.

Back to the examples - nowhere else, one encounters exotic and mind-blowing examples and counter examples other than in the world of mathematics! Mathematics is appreciated and advanced with great examples. There are books on pathological examples and counter examples alone. One of my favorite example is from elementary calculus - a function that is continuous everywhere, but differentiable nowhere. For more than a decade, world mathematicians believed such a function cannot exist - until a high school mathematics teacher, Karl Weierstrass (1815-97), constructed it. Soon after, he moved to a university.

Cantor Set is another mind-expanding example. It first provided an example of an uncountable set of measure zero. I understood their proofs only while studying real analysis. The beauty of these examples is that their graphs defy graphic capabilities of present technology as well as of the future to come! No other discipline can claim such 'futuristic' examples. **Mathematical insights are rightly attributed to the 'sixth' sense!**

Life is all about examples! In childhood, infants learn by imitation; as teens, they follow good examples and are inspired by examples; as adults, we emulate great minds. But, only a few create new examples and yet, fewer become examples to the rest of the world!

Mar 29, 2007/June, 2014

COMMENTS

This particular essay is so TRUE!!! A thought has more probability of being true if it is thought of independently by different people at different times. While cheering you on the various beautiful points raised, I want to emphasize that the sentences I have highlighted below in your letter is a conclusion I have come to after years of pondering about the attitudes of the US students (contrasting with taxi driving immigrant students) and the disrespect towards teachers and knowledge in general by both students and the general population, being so inconsistent with the sweep of the Nobel prizes by America.

Saying that the white man is practicing favoritism is too easy an escape!! This topic used to be a favorite topic of discussion in our Indian gatherings over the years and I have wasted quite a fraction of my life telling them that our Indian educational atmosphere is quite conducive to real learning etc., only to be booed down with the Nobel Prize situation. Only gradually did I realize that the composition of the U.S. population is in a continual flux due to immigration and to use a word like 'Americans' is to imply a static situation!! You hit the nail right on the head.

When the developing nations develop, the immigration patterns will consequently change and America has to follow the course of history with the rise and fall of civilizations. There is a book, which deserves to be better known with the approximate title of the decline of American education by Admiral Rickover. Please read it. He gave me such joy when he says the same things and suggests reading Gibbon's 'rise and fall of the roman empire'!!

Satish, we are correct in this. We are educators and we have been in the trenches and know the facts. But unfortunately, people don't realize that teaching is also a specialized profession, and the layman should not open his mouth and shoot off at random. Thanks and regards. **RAJA**

Satish, I really agree with your observations. Your point of view is further reinforced by an opinion piece in the Sunday, April 1 RJ written by a Western High School math teacher by the name of Barone, if I remember correctly. I'll try to send you a copy. **Dave Emerson**

MY A, B, C OF ALGEBRA

After all, what is Algebra? I got to tackle this question twice during the last couple of days. First it came in the context of *History of Mathematics* course (MAT 714) being taught this semester. The focus, during the week, was on the ancient history of Algebra. When history is dug deep into a thousand years, then the questions of authenticity of facts and evidence become very pertinent. Also, the concept of modern written record goes away. The archaeological projects, being most expensive, are beyond the means of even developing nations - **no** one would undertake it for the sake of ancient mathematics alone.

On checking the history of mathematics books published during the last 75 years, it is amazing to notice that there has been hardly any new evidence added to a little in circulation for decades. This is common to the history of China, India, Mesopotamia, and Egypt. Greek is an exception. Latin America and Africa are still in 'dark' ages as far as their ancient history is concerned.

Yesterday, my son-in-law proudly told me of his 9-year old daughter (from his previous marriage) placed in the 98th percentile of a national test. She being promising in math, he wanted her to jump start on Algebra. However, the little girl, accompanying the father, showed no interest in Algebra. It was a big social gathering and I took it as a challenge to 'open her mind to Algebra'. It reminds me of an anecdote in Einstein's life when a socialite lady, at a party, asked him to explain his 'hot' Theory of Relativity.

I am talking about Algebra as introduced in the 7th or 8th grade in schools. Geometry being visual and arithmetic so natural, that the symbols x, y and z used in algebra would naturally confound the kids initially. **Where is the heart of Algebra?** Algebra, if introduced as a natural 'generalization' of arithmetic, then its 'abstraction' is easily conveyed to the kids with examples; but never axiomatically.

Algebra was not my cup of tea the way it was poured in during the classes in my school days in India. There was absolutely no motivation for it. Its long division and pathological factorization problems overwhelmed the students. However, its application to 'age' problems proselytized me for ever. (Sample: ***Son's present age is one-fourth of father's age. After 24 years son's age will be half of the father's. What are their present ages?***) The joy of being able to do such problems is still vivid in my mind. Guess work is taken out. Algebraic approach is algorithmic and secular. Algebra gave us in India the same bragging rights that Calculus does it to high school students in the USA.

I wanted to make a point for Algebra in 5-7 minutes. Very casually, I asked her a series of questions like: How many total chairs are there, if one group has four chairs and the other has 3? Promptly, she said, 7 chairs. Pointing out at various other objects around us, I repeated the question with tables, spoons, plates, doors, pillars till she felt a little perplexed while answering them. I also changed the numbers with the objects.

Then I asked, "Is there anything common you see in these easy questions?" She took no time to realize that the numbers were important, not the objects. I said to myself that I made a point. Her father, listening to our conversation, expected for a grand appearance of Algebra at the end. There was no need for further reinforcement, as she had grasped the first leap into abstraction without hearing the word Algebra!

Algebra frees the kids from multiplication tables, though they are already out of fashion since the calculators have flooded the classrooms. Personally, once the basics of algebra were mastered, then there was never looking back to arithmetic.

Bringing a closure to the Relativity story, one must admit to Einstein's social ingenuity too, since he convinced the lady without recourse to any equations! The story goes on that once the lady was gratified, Einstein turned around to greet another lady! According to legends, Einstein never shied away from public adulation in the US as Gödel did. Incidentally, a UNLV physics professor regularly teaches a popular course on Special Theory of Relativity based upon Elementary Algebra only; no Calculus.

April 15, 2007

COMMENTS

Although, it may be too early, you have not mentioned if the young girl exhibited talents of a potential Nobel !! Or, did she say "Just tell me what to do". **RAJA**

While I was perplexed at the series of questions you were asking, I felt confident they had a purpose. Thank you for sharing the moral of the story through your reflection. It is difficult sometimes to push your children to learn a subject that the parent is not proficient in. While I have the ability to understand Algebra, it was never something I chose to do. I learned just enough to pass my classes and any college entrance exams I need to take. I appreciate your patience with teaching my daughter. I want her to continue thinking math is fun and her favorite subject. With so many negative opinions toward the subject, it is difficult to instill this love in your kids. I'm just fortunate that I married into a family with a math professor in it. Thanks Dad, **Alex**

FINAL EXAM FEVER

This time of academic semester is characterized with final exam fever in the US. However, its virus, confined amongst the students, dies out naturally after 2-3 weeks. In India, it lasts for at least two months. Moreover, no one remains immune from it, as it spreads beyond the student hostels - into the families at homes, business, and even movie theaters.

The word fever reminds me of the wisdom of my late father. Having studied Homeopathy, he practiced it on his large family of seven kids. During an infection with mild fever and no other symptoms, he would wait for a day or two before administering any medicine. He believed that the body cleanses itself through perspiration by raising its temperature when there is a minor internal imbalance.

The fever of the final exam has merits in stimulating the dormant brain cells. There is so much information on diet and exercise when it comes to sculpting various body muscles, but relatively very little towards the calisthenics of the brain. In math courses, regular homework, pop quizzes, hourly tests and a final comprehensive exam, each has its definite purpose. After all, an objective of learning any new material is that it be functional in future. But before it could be used, it must be retrievable from the brain. That is where different modes of testing and evaluation get into the picture.

Some of my students in the *History of Mathematics* (MAT 714) have been making a case for no Final Exam. Instead, they want a Take-Home exam. Take-Home Exam is perhaps an American curricular invention; unheard in India of my era of the 1950s. It never existed in the British education system; I am not sure about it in the French and German systems. As a matter of fact, the history of the (British) Cambridge Tripos Exams goes back to a few centuries and are known for their comprehensive formats and challenging problems.

Having worked in the US education system for nearly forty years, I must say that the Indian system of final exams that I took for my bachelor's were really brutal. The final exams at the end of the year carried everything - 100 % weight! It caused more depression and nervous breakdowns than I have known later in life. The pass percentage was generally less than 50%. Most failed students could re-take it only after one year - implying a colossal waste of time, talent and energy. The exams for the master's were similar, but limited to one discipline.

Over the years, my approach toward the final comprehensive exams has gradually changed according to the course level and the types of students. In 100-level courses, there is no exception to the comprehensive exam on the material covered from Day 1 to Day L. However, the weightage to the final exam varies from minimum of 20% in 100-level courses to maximum of 50% at 400-level modulo other considerations.

The lack of practice on the comprehensive final exams shows up in the US system at the time of 'comprehensive' written exams given for master's and PhD. For example, often, the students who have already passed the individual courses with A and B grades fail in the written exams when given over the same material! It is quizzical. Apart from the administration of written exams, there is a perennial nexus of faculty merit, student evaluation and inflated grades.

The comprehensive exams at the end of the semester prepare the students for the next math courses far better, particularly at the undergraduate level. On a personal note: due to my mental training in India for preparing and taking 4-6 three-hour exams at the end of every year, I was the only graduate student to pass all three 4-hour PhD Qualifying Exams in one shot at Indiana University, when they were first introduced in 1971. Earlier, it used to be all oral.

The best reward of written exam waits at the end when one has successfully passed it. **It is the highest point during studentship of knowing (not merely feeling) so much of material in life**. It is down the hill during the dissertation period! In any US university, written exams are unavoidable for doctorate in any area of mathematics!

April 28, 2007

COMMENTS

Extremely important observation. The final exams we had when in India, made me what I am. I had to get a total view of each subject and naturally I had to reflect on its connection with other subjects. This has stood me well for the rest of my life. I have always been appalled at the US students forgetting chapter 5, as we are starting chapter 7. They refuse to study 6.3 because the teacher said it won't be on the test. But then it has been pointed out that students in India also abuse the system and get through by 'mugging' or cramming during the last three months. But don't they come here and succeed? **RAJA**

How does one empty a set? There is a lot of recreation -- resembling competitive sport -- in the Tripos approach, but I have not a clue about the weight to assign it in evaluating an individual. This kind of mental recreation can be pleasant. I think that similar recreation is to be got from the riddle books of Raymond Smullyan. Even "non-mathematical types" can **play** with them for some pleasant and beneficial exercise. **Looy**

CALCULUS CHALLENGES YOU

Whether, teaching a first course on elementary calculus or taking it, it is far more than significant academically than any other course. The introduction of the power of the **Limit** concept and exposure to **Infinity** set this course apart from the rest. However, I do stress that the topics of precalculus are no less important. As a matter of fact, trigonometry and analytic geometry are far more useful than calculus in day-to-day operations.

Two weeks of the 5-week summer session are already gone, and two out of four major tests given out. It takes me two hours to write a 40-minute class test - since I make sure that the essential concepts, techniques and applications are all covered. Similar problems are avoided so that the students are not penalized again for the same mistakes. The bottom line is that if a student has not missed a class and has studied for at least two hours for each class hour, then he/she can finish my test in 25-30 minutes. I am against speed tests in mathematics at any level. Students are encouraged to give alternate solutions and review their work. The test problems are closely related with problems in the quizzes, homework and class discussions. At this fundamental level, there is no hide-and-seek game on choosing the test problems.

The student performance on the tests has been below my expectations. I never do any statistical analysis on test scores, as I get to know each one of my students in terms of their majors and background. The approach is customized and tailored. If one or two students show a sterling performance, I feel good overall! But no one scored 90% on the Second Test.

Las Vegas being the Entertainment Capital of the World, ten years ago, I felt incumbent to make mathematics instruction entertaining, but not to be laughed away! The clientele of calculus has changed 180 degree since I joined UNLV more than 30 years ago. In a class of 40, there is not even a single mathematics or physics major; only three in engineering! Nearly 50% of the students are from biology and chemistry; unheard years ago! Calculus winning new students is like all kinds of visitors coming to Las Vegas - 40 millions in 2006! Also, 50 % of the students are repeaters and 60 % working part/full time. Interestingly, there are only 5 freshmen, though it is a freshmen course for science/engineering students!

In disciplines – like, history, political science, biology and psychology, students are briefly exposed to the cutting edge of the issues, but elementary calculus is 300 years old. The frontiers of mathematics are not understood unless one has taken some graduate courses. It is the imperialistic nature of mathematics - in terms of new territories (applications) that defines all branches of mathematics. The new editions of precalculus and calculus textbooks primarily differ in terms of newer applications! The current *Finite Mathematics* textbook has a list of 200 applications.

A person teaching for over 30 years faces a bigger challenge in motivating the students. He can't get excited enough in his presentation by pointing out to a list of applications and word problems. **Unless mathematics has become of a paradigm in instructor's life, the freshness of lectures is likely to be missed by genuine students**. The not-so-genuine students simply want calculus 'out of their way'. In actuality, calculus puts them out of its way! No matter what are life's pursuits, mathematics is the best place to impart and imbibe the universal values of patience, preciseness, drill, discovery, problem analysis, and even ethical standards. So far, it has been a wonderful journey!

July 22, 2007/July 2014

COMMENTS

Why should we consider calculus or mathematics particularly suited to teaching ethics? During teaching I have indeed found that I make remarks on ethics. But I have considered it as part of my rambling (American style of teaching!!). It won't appear on the test!! Personally I consider it very valuable because the students are going to, in their later lives, forget differentiation anyway. Your thoughts! Regards. **RAJA**

I took calculus at St. Olaf College around fifty-four years ago, and have made little use of it since. I'm thinking it might be a good idea to sit through it again for a refresher, even though the classes I teach are far more elementary. My 122/123 classes turn out to be remedial for the majority of students, even though most of the content is lower level than algebra. There's a real trick to overcoming the aversion toward math that characterizes many students, and a similar aversion seems to be the norm in the sciences. It's not only socially acceptable among adolescents--- but even somewhat of a bragging point--- to say, "I'm just not a math/science person."

Your title is, "Calculus challenges you." It will only challenge those who step up to take the challenge. Unfortunately, it's also true that really basic math can be a challenge to many, but far too many sit through math classes with no real acceptance of the challenge. Somewhere between a third and a half of my students have taken algebra I and algebra II in high school, and then 095 and 096------but they still can't show an algebraic solution to a single variable word problem. That they got through earlier classes without learning simple problem solving techniques is a deplorable situation. I believe that a fair part of the problem lies in the use of multiple choice exams. I suggest that many students make "educated guesses" during a multiple choice exam more often that they pencil out a problem and then find their answer among the foils.

You mention alternate solutions, but those go out the window on Scantron-type exams. I'm also a proponent of partial credit, rather than black/white grading. Unless we eliminate the multiple choice exam, we give up the vital opportunity to see students as individuals----which follows naturally from careful grading of student exams. (If I had formal faculty status, I would propose elimination of graders throughout the department. If teaching is important, then grading student responses to your exams is too important to be done by any but the person teaching the class.) **Owen Nelson**

ON STUDENT CHEATING

Was I relieved yesterday, as I returned to my office and slumped into the chair! Two weeks ago, I decided to give the same test in both of my sections of a course that I am teaching this semester. The classes bring relatively large this year, and also a third course to be taken care, I felt a bit too much to write different tests for each section.

During the last 30+ years at UNLV, I have never taught two sections of the same course in one semester. Repeating lectures is not easy for me. Most instructors prefer multiple sections of the same course. It means only one preparation, and that does saves time. I remember a faculty member who used to teach three sections of the same course. Eventually, he wrote a successful textbook, which is not my cup of tea either!

The morning section ends at 9:45 AM and the afternoon begins at 1 PM. There are 42 students in the morning and 34 in the other. The students are mainly from two colleges - Hotel and Business. There is a strong probability that a student from afternoon section may be friendly with a student from the other. My name is posted for online registration. Hence the test problems and solutions may be passed on from the morning section to the afternoon one. The same tests must be avoided completely.

This concern for the integrity of the test is a natural outcome of my experience of teaching in India for seven years and in Malaysia for three years. There, the stories of creative and daring cheating before the tests, during the tests, and after the tests are fit for a TV serial. The system of examinations is also very different. Generally, the instructor who teaches a course, doesn't prepare the exam, does not make copies of the exam, does not proctor the exam, and does not even grade the exam. What a contrast with the US system of exams! In Indian system, at every stage, outsiders are involved in the name of integrity. Besides the students, parents and instructors are pulled into these nefarious acts. Consequently, conducting final exams has turned into a big law and order national problem.

A sigh of relief came when my grader reported the scores of each class. The average, highest, lowest scores and standard deviations were nearly the same! In excitement, I shared this story with a US-born colleague. He was not surprised at all. On the other hand, he surprised me by telling that he had been giving the same exam semester after semester! In fact, he has the solutions of exam problems posted on his web site. Yet, it makes no difference in students' performance. It appears that the fast life styles of UNLV students do not leave them any time for such academic infractions.

Having taught in different cultures, I am totally convinced of general integrity of the US students. Moreover, it is a reflection of relative honesty prevailing in the offices, businesses, and in every walk of public life. I must stress it is relative. Five years ago, I caught the first cheater who happened to be a foreign student from Indian subcontinent! It was during the second test. He raised my suspicion by his perfect score on the first test. However, during class participation, he seldom answered correctly.

An irony of this scenario is that despite relatively low incidence of cheating, UNLV has developed a very comprehensive policy on cheating and plagiarism, and has created an office for it! To the best of my knowledge, hardly any Indian college or university would come close to it. The funny thing is who cares, even if it is there! Back to square one, will I give the same tests again? With my state of mind and experience, no anxiety is worth having it. Besides, even if one student takes advantage of it, it is not right to let it go.

Feb 13, 2008/July, 2014

COMMENTS

Nana you are every student's dream professor- one who is too lazy to change the tests between classes! Just change a few numbers and then you can't cheat as easy, you would still need to know how to work out the problem. Did I tell you I got an A- in my Differential Equations class last quarter! And everyone says it's the hardest out of all the other lower division math courses. **Anjali**

KEEP YOUR TEXTBOOKS!

Two days ago, I passionately remarked in my *College Algebra* class (MATH 124), "**Mathematics textbooks are like red wine, as they too get better with time!**" The students naturally burst out with oohs, ahas and laughters. The context was some discussion on a recently identified national trend amongst the undergraduate mathematics students who do not seriously study their textbooks. It was time to capitalize on this moment before my remark was forgotten.

College Algebra is a freshmen course, but 80% of the students are sophomores and juniors. They already have taken a lot of other courses. UNLV students are mature. That was good for making a point, "The textbooks of courses in English, computer science, psychology, sociology, history, political science, business etc. have little re-sale values, as most likely, they are going to be changed next semester. Their value is reduced to zero after a few years. The main reason being, these subjects thrive on theories that change with persons, places and time. Mathematics is independent of these variables. Theorems in mathematics never change; however, their generalization is an altogether a different intellectual exercise."

The story, I said, was no different in sciences and engineering. New stars, nano particles, bacteria, chemicals are being discovered everyday, and that need to be incorporated in the textbooks. That is a selling point for the adoption of new textbooks. Mathematics in *College Algebra* is 300 years old, but its applications are being discovered everyday! That alone is a reason for new editions of undergraduate textbooks. **Mathematics is a kind of ultimate colonizer in the world of knowledge!**

For years, I saved not only the textbooks, but also, my class notes. Just like one picks up a dictionary to check on a difficult word, one goes to an old math textbook for a forgotten formula. Old textbooks make common sights in homes and offices. A friend's family room has all the science and math books used by their four kids who studied in the same private high school! My son, who took calculus 22 years ago, occasionally refers to his *Calculus* textbook by Ellis & Gullick.

My remark has a strange coincidence with Yahoo news today. It is reported that a Chinese billionaire paid $500,000 for 27 rare red wine bottles! One may be surprised with the dollar figure, but not with the value of ageing wines. During WW II, once the Nazis occupied France, one of the first seizures was the rare French wine cellars!

The correlation coefficient between ageing wine and ageing math books may be small. Math textbooks rarely lose in value. In 1994, Bill Gates, the world's richest man, paid staggering 30 million dollars for Leonardo de Vinci's 15th century rare manuscript, ***Codex Leicester***! That says it all.

A student remarked, what is the point of keeping a textbook for applications that will become old? I said, "**Today, you are learning the formulas and their latest applications. Tomorrow, you may need to refer to a formula, when new situations stir for it**." Students giving suggestions for enhancing the use of textbooks (priced at $125), shall earn extra credits, I added.

Apr 19, 2008/July, 2014

COMMENTS

Interesting. I'm currently using the second edition of Dugoposki's *Elementary & Intermediate Algebra* at University of Phoenix. The courses are similar to 095 & 096, but they're the basic math requirement at UOP. They used the first edition, too, and the second has some major changes from the first. The third is out now. I have it, but it's not yet in use at UOP. The third is quite similar to the second. I would expect that future editions won't have great changes, either.

My role in this is mostly tutoring, so I see syllabi from many different Profs. One never assigns any of the word problems (applications), and he says it's because students have such difficulty with them. Others assign just one or two from a problem set, and some of their students simply skip them. At the other extreme are a few Profs whose assignments are 30-40 % application problems and they also make it clear that they are not to be skipped over.

My preference is for the latter approach, because the texts we have today are getting more and more good problems that show how math is useful in the real world, something that is a missing element for many students. Over the past half dozen years, I have often offered students an extra-credit point bonus for describing a situation where they have made use of algebra in their daily lives. Most are unable to come up with anything at all. I always provide several examples, but the overall results seem to indicate that math is, to many, just something they have to study-----but they don't see much use for it in their lives. **ONN**

ENOUGH OF COLLEGE ALGEBRA!

"Please make a change in my fall teaching schedule from College Algebra (MATH 124) to Precalculus I (MATH 126)," I wrote the Associate Chair; "Reason: teaching two sections of College Algebra to nearly 80 students this semester has been too much." Did I ask for them? No. In addition to Calculus III, these sections fell into my lap due to some mis-communication. I seldom complain about my teaching assignment. My professional forte does lie in teaching variety of courses.

Over the years, I have started taking lower-division teaching as a sort of performance too. After all, UNLV sits in the heart of Las Vegas, the **Entertainment Capital of the World**. Most students work in the casino industry. Yes, my lectures include developing students' appreciation for math and minimizing their math anxiety which is high amongst the college algebra students. A good performance is always emotional, and excitement is integral in my teaching style through class participation.

Here is a rub that is gradually being observed. My 'house' is never full. About the legendary Elvis Presley, it is said, that he never sang to an empty seat in a showroom. My brother-in-law, working in Las Vegas Hilton then, tells stories of Elvis sellouts. Only a few entertainers can boast of such a record. In college, teaching a math course, like college algebra, and shooting for this standard, is a far cry. All the students may not come everyday, everyone may not enjoy my lectures, but I try to live upto this benchmark. It keeps me professionally active, physically agile, and mentally alert. What more can one ask for in return?

In any endeavor of life, a situational saturation point is reached. Then, one digs into an old bag for new tricks for re-energization. At times, it seems, **Students' Response** $= \sqrt{My\ Enthusiasm}$! Some of the quizzes, motivational approaches, and extra credit assignments, were never tried before. By the way, the first time I taught this course was in spring 1975, and last, in fall 1990. In all, it has been taught seven times. In 1990, I told the chairman, "On a regular basis, College Algebra should be taught by graduate assistants or part-time instructors, as it is the under-utilization of faculty expertise with PhDs." Without a change in mindset, it is very challenging, in general, for research-oriented faculty to communicate mathematics at this level, week after week.

College Algebra is defined by tremendous heterogeneity in terms of class standing, age groups, and majors. Above all, the time of perquisites taken may vary from one semester to 20 semesters ago! Precalculus I (MATH 126) is a parallel course for students going into areas of science, engineering and education. College Algebra, offered in maximum number of sections (20), is bread and butter of the Department, College, and University. Students are drawn from the colleges of business, hotel, urban affairs and nursing. Prerequisites being the same, the dual credits are not permitted for the two. Precalculus I would provide a fresh comparison between the two groups of students – which I like to see once in a while.

During one of the reflective moments, it struck me that one cannot hold intellectual 'erection' semester after semester. It reminds me of a classic joke of a sex starved wife of a farmer. Naggingly, she said, "Look, how does a bull get fired up at the sight of a cow?" The husband retorted," Because, he charges into a different cow each time!" I have yet to repeat my teaching schedule from one semester to the next.

May 01, 2008/July, 2014

PERSONAL REMARKS

TIPS TO PASS CALCULUS III

In the US, the sources of advice have gone upside down. In the fast pace of US life, there is little regards for advice from the parents and teachers. On the other extreme, the rapists advise how to avoid being raped; burglars dispense tips on how to make the house burglar proof, and so on. In particular, it seems my expertise of 40+ years in college teaching is out of date, or irrelevant.

Therefore, given below are the pieces of advice from my 35 students who took Calculus III in Spring-2008. I specifically asked them, "If you have to give one of two words of advice to a fellow student who is planning to take this course from me, then just write it down." Most of the following suggestions have been given by more than one student!

1. Do the homework before the class; you will understand it better.
2. Practice again after the class. At least, do even a little math every day so that you won't forget.
3. Do every problem in the book, even if they are not assigned, because they might be on a test.
4. Ask someone for help because a lot this stuff is confusing. Concepts build up on each other.
5. Study test and quiz problems most. They come again and are important.
6. Do the HW on the same day that you learnt the material.
7. Use the study guide that comes with the textbook.
8. Read the book and understand the concepts of each section in each chapter.
9. When doing problems, understand each problem and do similar problems.
10. Get lots of sleep. Do not pull all nighters. Master your notes, and you will master your class. This means you must attend class.
11. Look over all examples problems in the textbook.
12. Read the sections before the class and take your own notes.
13. If you have trouble with the material, get a tutor.
14. Do extra credit assignments.
15. Learn to love math as well. If you find it interesting, then you will grasp it quicker.

16. Don't procrastinate until the last minute.
17. Make sure you don't just glance over the material, but instead, read your book thoroughly.
18. Enjoy your professor, he is funny, and do your best not to fall asleep during class. He is very generous on giving extra credits, but you must put in the effort to get it done.
19. Ask questions that you didn't understand.
20. Look around to your left, right, front and back, find some one you know!! If you don't know any one, then get off your butts and meet some one. Try to have common goals so you can accomplish more together and ask each other when the professor may not be available.
21. Start preparing for the exam two weeks (during a semester) in advance.
22. Befriend your classmate and instructor. They will make class enjoyable and more beneficial. Good luck!
23. Do the HW even though it isn't worth a lot of points, it forces you to learn the material, and test questions are usually similar to homework problems (some with quiz problems)

Now choose any 10 out of 23 positively tested ideas, and you pass. It can be done in 3,432,198 ways!!

July 05, 2008/July, 2104

INSTRUCTOR'S SUPPLEMENT

1. No formal reviewing before the test or quiz. Reviewing is neither repeating the lectures, nor working out the problems likely to be on the test.
2. Concepts and techniques are more important than a few specific problems.
3. Reviewing is continuous study habit in the confines of your study.
4. Only during a regular semester for the Comprehensive final, a day of reviewing is set aside.
5. New material may be covered even a day before the test.
6. Your attendance, attention and concentration in the class are very crucial.
7. There is too much material in the course and I don't want you to go underprepared for the next course.
8. The test time is fine-tuned. If you ever feel the time is not enough for a test/quiz, then it simply means that you have not devoted enough time before the test. A rule of thumb is two hours for every class hour during the same day.
9. Always give your self-practice tests.
10. Make sure you are able to review the entire test material before test.

IS IT A MELTDOWN OF ......?

Today, before covering **Synthetic Division** in a standard *College Algebra* course (MATH 124), I quizzed the students on a simple long division problem - namely, $x-2) \, 2x^3 - 5x^2 - 2x + 5$. For the fun of it, I also added a problem on the division of integers, $2\,7\,6) \, 1\,9\,3\,7\,6\,9$. A simple instruction was to find the quotients and remainders in each case without the use of a calculator. Being a bonus quiz, it had no negative effect on the grades. Out of 31 students, only one got the algebraic division right, and ten had no idea on the 5th Grade arithmetic division!

The prerequisites for this course include a remedial course, *Intermediate Algebra* (MATH 096) or **three years** of high school math at the level of algebra, or above. As a matter of fact, long division is introduced in another remedial course, *Elementary Algebra* (MATH 095). These remedial courses, not existing in the US colleges 50 years ago, are now regular courses. At UNLV, however, they do not count towards graduation. Several sections of remedial courses are offered each session to meet the growing demands of all kinds of students. Besides servicing the students, it is a good business for the colleges.

Math instructors commonly share such stories for mutual amusement or disenchantment. But this scenario struck a deeper cord in my mind. Is it a meltdown of mathematics corresponding to the meltdown of the US economy - making headlines for the last couple of years? The housing industry is the engine of the US economy. The affordable housing was so much politicized that individuals and institutions got loans upon loans – a few, perhaps, 100 times of what they could afford.

The closure of some name banks, including 158-year old Lehman Brothers, made me think of iconic universities like Harvard and Stanford closing their doors one day. For the last 20 years, college education has prominently entered into presidential elections. It must be affordable! That means giving out student loans to undeserving students, softer admission standards, but expecting higher retention and graduation rates. It is a recipe for busting the great American higher education.

The writings on the walls have been there for the last 2-3 decades. In 34 years at UNLV, the falling college standards are partly due to students' commitment to their jobs, families, and social obligations over the courses. No matter how enthusiastic one is about teaching, but encountering unprepared students semester after semester, is bound to lower instructors' mathematical abilities too.

Affordable housing, affordable college education, affordable medicine, and affordable insurances, are buzz words of greed, diminishing individual initiative, and disguised socialism. The American Dream is realized with hard work and honesty. Now, it is becoming a social responsibility. Uncle Sam must provide everything. The last straw is the 'affordable' immigration and US citizenship. It is ironic that during this election campaign, no presidential candidate has uttered even a single word against the illegals in the US. It shocks me as I entered the US legally on a student visa.

A lesson of history is that every great nation and civilization first collapses from within. We may be witnessing the beginning of the meltdown of America. Despite inevitability of the fall of a great civilization, it can be slowed down by men and women of vision and self-sacrifice.

Sep 30, 2008/July, 2014

COMMENTS

The civilization collapses when its leaders do not have vision, but on top of it, they are obstinate. There is a big difference between resolve and obstinacy. Current administration's policies on all fronts domestic or foreign have done irreparable damage to USA. History will look at Bush to be the President who led to rapid start of the end of American Empire. Even McCain and Palin in their debates try to run away from Bush record. They are becoming agents for change from what, Bush policies of course. How sad.

Unbridled Capitalism and greed are also leading to collapse of this country. The subprime loans were not given because of socialistic idea but because of greed. There needs to be balance between capitalism and socialism. Both systems have pros and cons. When one lives in a community a society then socialism does play a role. People on right give all kinds of socialism a bad name to grind their axe. **Rahul** (MD)

Yikes....I have copied this to Ann McDonough.... **Neal Smatresk** (Provost, UNLV)

I'm so profoundly grateful we have the Academic Success Center!!! **Ann Macdonough** (Dean)

Agreed. But I wonder if standards have dropped perceptively or our memories are imprecise. When I joined UNLV in 1971, Vietnam veterans were crowding back - and they were a bad lot; standards seemed abysmally low to me. Students' capabilities and performance seemed to rise slowly over the ensuing years. I wonder now if my standards had dropped at the time or if students got better. I suspect the latter. I started teaching upper division and graduate courses and continued over the years, then in my last year, I taught freshmen and sophomores and their lack of preparation and plain dumbness were a shock. It gave me a retrospective appreciation of the whole educational process. **Robert W Moore** (Retired UNLV Management Professor)

Beautifully written--I couldn't agree more! I've seen the same thing, but in less years! **Aaron Harris**

FIRST DAY AT UNIVERSITY OF NIZWA

"There are no dull moments here," quipped Sue Monroe. It was a week ago, when I stopped to say her hello in the same hallway offices. Sue is a Canadian working in English Department. The closest place she has been to Las Vegas was during a trip to a neighboring state, Utah. Today, stopping by her office again, I told her, "Sue, what you said a week ago, is more than a truism." That brought a smile on her face.

I am writing this *Reflection* while sitting in a 30-capacity classroom assigned for a *Group Theory* course, (MATH 310) expected to draw about 10 students. I never sit down in a chair while teaching. Mathematics is a dynamic activity. The students must not have their backs leaning on any support, and instructors must remain on their feet writing on the boards, or walking up and down helping the students struggling at certain points during lectures. This physical exercise comes as bonus to math instructors only.

Today is Saturday, like Monday in the non-Muslim world, and it is the first day of classes in the University of Nizwa (UN), Oman. This is also the first day of spring semester at the UN. Not even a single student has come to the class! I came pepped up for it 5 minutes before the class to alleviate students' first-day confusion about classrooms, instructors, and courses work etc. The first thing done is to write the basic information about the course and instructor on the board for the students to read before they settle down in their seats.

Well, when no one came in the next 10 minutes, my mind started galloping for a *Reflection*. Here it is on a roll! It has been 30 minutes already. I could go back to my office, but I stayed on here for a couple for reasons. The main one being, that I was told by a colleague that instructors are 'monitored' here. It sounds like some places in the US, where PC browsers are snooped to discourage faculty from viewing porn in their offices! Well, the comparison may be far-fetched and debatable.

However, I am working on this *Reflection* in the classroom with open doors for everyone to see me sitting. I do stand out unique on a small

UN campus for my dress and features in a mass of people where men wear long white full sleeve Arabian outfit (*dishdash*) that goes with typical Omani caps, or headwears, (*Mosar* and *Komah*) that look like mini Indian *pagris* of rural Rajasthan or Gujarat.

A bunch of girls in black flowing and sweeping robes (*Abaya* = *Burqua* minus veil) were about to enter when one of them noted the room number G, not C. Yes, the capital G is seen without a horizontal dash on the vertical bar. As a corollary, English learning and teaching are a big business in the Gulf countries. In Oman, public signs are both in Arabic and English. Incidentally, India has gone too far in English, where language institutes advertise American English and British English; but Australian English is no where.

At the UN, the largest number of students are in two English Programs, far away from English literature and composition. Every student has to pass **TOEFL** for graduation and getting a government job! Instructors are from several English-speaking countries. The UN itself is modeled after a campus of University of Wisconsin in terms of its administrative structure, courses, programs etc.

Most textbooks are American. But students do not buy them. Interestingly, it is the duty of the instructors to issue textbooks to the students at the beginning of the semester, collect them at the end of the course, and have them delivered back to the warehouse. It is unimaginable in the US. After all, you can transplant only one organ at a time from one body to the other! Today, the Dept Secretary being on leave, the Dept Head (not elected Chair) 'issued' me a board eraser and color markers. About the desk copies for my use, he politely suggested not to write anything on the pages, though the two books were already heavily scribbled! Instructors have to return their desk copies too.

Well, the attendance story was repeated exactly for the second course, *Number Theory* (MATH 340), in the afternoon. On checking with other colleagues, the attendance numbers were in ones and twos. A part of the reason is that this week is for dropping/adding courses. You cannot transfer a system completely without changing the mindsets, and that inherently is a function of religious beliefs, traditions, and customs in these ancient societies.

Things are no different in India, less than 1000 miles east of Oman. I recently learnt about similar academic laxity from my niece studying in Pune, one of the greatest hubs for all kinds of educational institutions in India.

However, this story will not be complete without connecting it with an 'interesting' morning episode. Having missed the 7 AM campus bus, butterflies started flying about being on time. I repeatedly called 2-3 persons that I only know so far. While sitting in the hotel lobby, I noted a lady in waiting too. On introducing, Noore, a new hire like me, but from Malaysia, was also waiting for her college bus. Around 8:40, we hopped in a bus. But on reaching the place, it was not the UN campus!

Noore works in a different institution altogether, but not too far from the UN. After our struggle with Arabic, and of the natives with English, I was finally driven to the UN campus at 9:30 AM, late by 30 minutes for the first class on the first day - never happened before! Quickly, it was discovered that the course time was changed from 9 to 10 AM without informing me. What a relief!

At the end of the day, I realized abundance of public and institutional conveniences that the Americans take for granted, as if they are universal. Every time, I return to the USA from overseas, I appreciate what the US life offers. One never forgets the first experiences, but this day at the UN will stand out for a while.

Jan 24, 2009 (Oman)/Feb, 2010

ONE DOWN, AND......!

The US has set the benchmarks in every aspect of life. Most of them are subtle, invisible, and taken for guaranteed. However, they prominently surface up when one goes overseas. It struck me, as I was going through the first week of instruction at the University of Nizwa (UN), Oman. Five years ago, this university was set up on a model of University of Wisconsin campus. On papers, its administrative structure, degree programs, academic calendars etc. are isomorphic to a typical 4-year college and university in the US.

Oman is an Islamic Sultanate (monarchy), where Thursday and Friday make a weekend. In other words, Saturday is the first working day! From a mathematical point of view, it is a shift operation; either forward by five days, or backward by two days. The class schedules are like those in a typical US university - standard 3-credit courses are taught on three days or two days a week.

It was a shocker, when not even a single student came on the first day of classes in all of my three courses. It reminded me of some instructors at UNLV, who have their individual attendance policies printed in the class schedules – one of them – 'a student missing the first day of classes will be dropped from the course'. It seems an American academic system, transplanted in some cultures, takes time for its full acceptance. However, no judgment is intended at one social milieu over the other. It is the new perspectives on life that I seek out for keeping me energized overall.

Out of the eight classes in the first week, only one student came in two of them, and four in the other. As a matter of fact, I missed a Monday afternoon class myself! The SMW lost its 'alignment', since it just did not click on me, that I had to be in a class at that particular hour. It was realized on Wednesday, when a student told me, how she alone waited in the classroom! I felt so bad, as it never happened before. It is not the *Law of Large Numbers* that caught on me, but the years of mental conditioning.

Fortunately, in the first week, I did not have to worry about my board and lodging, since I was put up in a nice hotel. I will move when a furnished accommodation is provided. Here furnished accommodation means no pillows, sheets, blankets, towels; pots, pans, cutlery; cleansers, sponges, mops and brooms. Who wants gathering of these household hassles while visiting for a semester, or two? The one accommodation shown last week, was not acceptable.

UN is located in a small temporary campus. Nearly 100% faculty and deans are expatriates. We are already comparing notes on varied experiences. In particular, we often talk about a big gap between the course syllabi submitted by the faculty and what the students are capable of understanding It is all due to students' weak high school background and their difficulties with English comprehension.

Nevertheless, it is good to set high individual and institutional goals. In contrast, the US public high schools have been lowering their standards in order to meet the lowest common denominators in the society. Oman has only opened the first pages of its book on modern education.

Jan 30, 2009 (Oman) July, 2014

COMMENTS

Amazing experience. You are adventurous. Keep up your thoughts and observations. Your second-hand experiences are edifying. **Robert W Moore**

Dear Mr. Bhatnagar, I am really thankful to you for some informative pages you are forwarding to me. I may not reply to every piece you send across to me. Nevertheless, I am thoroughly enjoying them. Regards, **Narayana Joisa,** Principal of India high school in Nizwa.

PLAYING IT OUT

When a person runs after new cultural and academic experiences, then one is bound to encounter a mix of pleasant and not-so-pleasant situations. For instance, this is the ending of the 3rd week in a *Linear Algebra II* (Math 365) course, at University of Nizwa (UN). The textbook, like in all other courses, is American, by David Lay. The classes meet twice a week for 75 minutes on Sundays and Tuesdays. Yes, Thursdays and Fridays are the weekends.

Yesterday, at the end of the period, as I started distributing a 5-minute quiz based upon the previous lecture, the students started saying, no, no; and pleaded for no quiz. There being 19 students including only one male, two girls stood up and started urging the others in Arabic to stop taking the quiz and walk out. Politely and firmly I said, "Those not taking it will get zero on this quiz." Still, all except four students left the classroom murmuring.

Now here is a rub from my perspective. These students are all seniors and some are graduating by the end of this semester, or summer. Nearly one-half of them are math majors and the other half math education. From the US perspective, such a class attitude and behavior is almost non-existent. Certainly, this scenario is common with 'neighboring' India, where the students make media headlines by walking out of the final exams on flimsy pretexts. Scheduling exams is a nightmare for the administrators in India. I know it, as I studied and taught in India till the age of 29, and continue to visit it every year.

Coming back to my UN students, they were informed in week #1 and #2 that they should be ready for weekly quizzes. Since only one student came on the second meeting of the 1st week, the first quiz was given out in the second week. To alleviate some quiz anxiety, it was a two-student team quiz. The idea is to encourage peer learning too. Today's quiz was open notes only. It stresses upon punctuality, regular attendance and right note taking. The formats of my quizzes do have a touch of creativity.

Despite this episode, I am sympathetic toward these students. Their English is a hindrance in understanding mathematics. Most of them started learning it only 4-5 years ago. Last week, I asked them to read 3-4 lines of a handout. It was atrocious, hardly better than that of second graders in the US Elementary schools, when it comes to enunciation and comprehension.

At the UN, before taking regular courses, the students have to take one year of immersion in English only, and pass the TOEFL at a score of 500 or above! It is a torture for them. However, this is what the Omani Government wants. In public places, the hoarding signs are both in Arabic and English.

Above all, their study habits reflect a culture; no judgment is implied. I am often reminded to lower my expectations and do more examples. Thinking is a mere word, since they grow up memorizing and taking/giving orders. Despite these boundary conditions, my UN experience will be worth it if only one student can be turned on to mathematical thinking.

Feb 11, 2009 (Oman)

COMMENTS

Wow, and I thought Americans were the worst behavior on record!!! I guess I shouldn't complain anymore... Really interesting insights, if I were to teach college someday I would love to have a visiting professor experience too. Cheers, **Aaron**

ADVICE TO MY OMANI STUDENTS

As I was grading the three tests given last week in three courses, I went through a wave of observations on your learning curve in general, and of mathematics, in particular. Certainly, I am getting lot of new experiences in academics and beyond for which I came from UNLV to the University of Nizwa (UN).

Since the UN started in 2004, some of you may be in the first graduating class of 2009. However, it raises a basic question: **What is the value of your bachelor's diploma**? For instance, the Central Bank of Oman stands behind the paper bills of Omani Rials. In order to find your academic worth, the GRE must be taken. It is like TOEFL for English.

Your lack of command over English is obstructing your learning of mathematics. It is shocking to note poor enunciation of common English words, limited grammar, vocabulary, and inability to write even one correct sentence after four years! It is high time that the UN Administration evaluates this English teaching product. Otherwise, the English mission of the Sultanate and UN is not going to be fulfilled.

I have advised and encouraged you not to mix English with Arabic, when necessary, while speaking with each other in the class or outside. At the College meeting, the Dean clearly told the faculty that English was the medium of instruction. The Arabic faculty members teaching and speaking with you in Arabic in their offices and classes are making your learning problems worse.

Since the beginning of the semester, I told you that a rule of thumb on study habits is to find **at least two hours for every hour of class instruction, and on the same day**. However, some of you walk into the classes drawing blanks on the previous materials. The six-week homework that most of you turned in was not even one-day of reviewing done before an exam!

Sitting with crossed hands and reclined back are unprecedented scenes in math classes. It seems that after four years at UN, you are still living in high school mindsets. That is why, perhaps, most of you continue to address me as 'teacher'. You have no idea what it takes to get a PhD in mathematics and become a professor in an American university.

Also, it seems as if the prerequisite courses were never taken! One may not remember everything of a math course taken a semester ago, but one never forgets everything either! One reason is that you do not own math textbooks. After three years of math -including foundations of math, most of you have no concept of a proof and how it is different from verification, and counterexamples.

The American way of learning and teaching are different from the ways done in India, Philippines and Middle East. I found it out when I left India for PhD at Indiana University (USA). The academic shift, from imitating solutions to independent problem-solving, was a shocker to me. Nevertheless, the UN is based on a US university model.

Generally, periodic exams tell a lot about problems that are not in one's knowledge, or plain misconstrued. It can apply to one's health during a routine check-up or about a car when diagnostic tests are run on it. Academic quizzes/exams also serve similar purposes on your understanding of the material. Take self-tests in life more often!

March 11, 2009(Oman)/ July, 2014

BETTER TO BE PRO-ACTIVE

Dear Colleagues: This reflective note is being written in the same spirit in which I introduced myself at the College Meeting. We may have come from different parts of the world, but our common mission is to make this newly 'born' (2004) University of Nizwa (UN) a better place than we found it. This thought is taken from Rabindranath Tagore, 1913-Nobel Laureate in literature, and the founder of Shantiniketan University. Once, addressing the newly hired faculty, he said, **"Take away what is best in Shantiniketan, and leave your best here."** Enhancing and reinforcing the academics standards is the call of the hour at the UN.

This note is prompted by some thoughts generated while grading three class tests (50/75 Mts.) given last week. The weekly 5-minute quizzes did provide me some ideas on students' poor study habits and weak backgrounds. But I gave them some benefit, as in this part of the world - including Indian subcontinent, students don't study everyday, unless the final exams are close.

I have a unique 'distinction' of getting MS from India, researching for two years towards PhD in India. After teaching for seven years in four institutions in India, I went to Indiana University, Bloomington in 1968 for an American PhD. The two education systems are poles apart. Nevertheless, let me add that the US undergraduate education is envy of the world today.

The students in *Introduction to Group Theory* (Math 310), *Elementary Number Theory* (Math 340) and *Linear Algebra II* (Math 365) are all graduating seniors, that is, in their 5th year. In 2009, some students may be the in first graduating class of the UN. Here is **a tip of an iceberg** of their comprehension of mathematics, at this stage:

1. $(2k + 1) = (K + 1)^2$; $(2k + 1)^2 = 4K^2 + 1$; $n^2 + 4 = (n^2 + 2)(n^2 - 2)$.

    As someone put it, that such errors are not committed even in one's dream!

2. The Principle of Mathematical Induction is not fully understood even by a single student while doing a simple problem of proving: $1 + 3 + 5 + \ldots\ldots\ldots + (2n - 1) = n^2$.

3. How can anyone understand, much less, apply any mathematical topic without understanding definitions and statements (not proofs) of important theorems? Since Day Number One, definitions are stressed and quizzed on, and yet, on the tests, nearly every student was blown away. They continue to think that verification is a proof.

4. In *Group Theory*, the students cannot just leap into its abstract nature, whether it is arbitrary binary operation, equivalence relations, or subgroups. They are deeply embedded into the real numbers and their properties.

5. In *Linear Algebra II*, abstraction again is a big problem while dealing with general linear transformations and abstract vector spaces. They are stuck with vectors in R^n only!

6. It seems that prerequisites of the courses are irrelevant to these students. No one forgets everything of a course taken a semester or two ago. In order to alleviate it, the students must be able to buy their textbooks during pre-registration periods, so that they have them before the semester begins.

I hate bashing my students, as it is like bashing my own kids. However, the underlying objective is to help the students to achieve their potentials. We have to accept these students, as faculty has little control over their admission. Nevertheless, the faculty recommendations can eventually make a difference in future crops of students.

7. One clear reason of students' problems with math lies in their lack of comprehension and command over oral and written English. They do not understand commonly used terms in English, the declared medium of instruction at the UN.

While mixing Arabic with English during lectures and in the offices may help students for a moment, but in the long run, it will be counterproductive. Faculty has control over these parameters.

8. The current math requirements for bachelor's degree are too strong for these students with weak backgrounds and no history. Many colleges in the US, including my own UNLV, have less credit requirements for math majors. It is worth revising.

9. My big suggestion is that before graduating from the UN, the students must take the GRE exam; general and subject parts. It is like TOEFL at the entry time in a program. It will bring an international validation to the all undergraduate programs.

10. In conclusion, I must add another side of students. The UN administration seems super sensitive to students' concern (95 % being females). They can directly go to a Department Head, Dean, or even the Chancellor without discussing their issues with the faculty members concerned. It breaks down the line of authority, and consequently dilutes the academic standards.

Am I frustrated over the scenario described? Not the least; rather, I am genuinely sympathetic towards these students mathematically! In mathematics courses, these students are like 100-Lbs weaklings trying to lift up 200 Lbs.

The UN is a baby institution; it can lay down groundwork for solid traditions and practices. Therefore, the Math Faculty should discuss these issues, and make periodic recommendations to the Administration. At UNLV, every new program undergoes an intensive review after five years. The UN, created on a model of University of Wisconsin campus, is ripe for a comprehensive review.

Thanks for your considerations.

March 14, 2009

A WAY TO LEARN MATHEMATICS

There is an aha moment in every aspect of life, provided the mind remains fully engaged in figuring out solution of a problem. At University of Nizwa (UN), my challenge has been to make the students think about solving a problem. Last week, a straight textbook example was on a 5-minute quiz. Since no one got it right, it was put on a test at the following meeting, after replacing a_1, a_2, a_3 with b, c, a respectively. A height of memorization without understanding is that most students used the subscripts, but not the given a, b and c.

The UN students are far more different that I have ever encountered. In the beginning, the Department Head told me, "Satish, do more examples." Already, the American textbooks, used here, have too many examples thus overwhelming the students before exercises. Even for spoon-feeding, one has to open the mouth before the food can be placed in.

In my three math courses, there are 25 students including only one male. Some are taking one or two courses, but one student is in all three of them. Repeatedly, I tell them 'that you can ask any question, but there is only one condition—you must bring the worksheets where you have tried the problem(s), as it would tell me precisely where you are stuck'. Fewer students have come to me!

My teaching style is participatory. Discussing a problem is like solving it by an assembly line approach. Here, I daily feel 'stonewalled'. These girls simply refuse to take any initiative in writing the next step or verbalize it. Instead of getting frustrated, my curiosity is whetted as to how these students learn mathematics, if they learn any of it at all.

Said, a colleague (from Egypt) and I share an office. Lot more students come to him for help. He works out a solution while sitting at his desk and 2-3 students (90 % of the UN students are females) stand across, or by his side. Said speaks out in Arabic as he works out problems. The students seem to 'recite' mathematical steps after him. They can't read it clearly, much less understand it, when seen perpendicular to the lines of writing.

Suddenly, these pieces of students' learning of mathematics fell into place for me. **It is the Quranic influence on learning**. Since the age of 7, the Muslim kids are encouraged to memorize the verses of their holy Quran by recitation after a qualified clergy. Quranic Arabic, not being a street language; comprehension is beyond the young minds.

The Chinese learn by memorization too. Nearly 20,000 ideographs of Chinese language have to be memorized for learning it. Twenty years ago, a research study in mathematics education explained why the Chinese college students perform better than other ethnic groups in Malaysia. It was attributed to the Chinese ability to memorize.

Today, I shared this insight with a Muslim colleague in mathematics from Iraq and another Muslim colleague in education from Kenya. Indians, in general, learn by multiple revisions. During college days, (1955-59), a classmate reviewed all textbook exercises 4-5 times before the final exam, which is given at the end of every two years. At the other extreme, the Americans learn math by thinking.

April 26, 2009 (Oman)

COMMENTS

It is interesting that the research study found that Chinese students in Malaysia did well in Maths due to their ability to memorize. I always thought that they were generally better in Maths since the Chinese primary school syllabus covers higher level math topics at an earlier stage compared to our normal national primary schools. As such, Chinese school students learn more advance topics and are able to solve more complex problems at a younger age! So they well ahead of other students when they enter college together with other students!

I empathize with you on your frustration in teaching the UN students. It is a pity that they are not taking much initiative to learn from you. I really enjoyed your classes and listening to your experiences of teaching students in India and the US! It helped open up my mind to the world beyond Malaysia! Regards, **Gayathri**

PERSONAL REMARKS

A PARTING NOTE

(A reflective farewell to my Students in the University of Nizwa)

On the 3rd of June, I will be back in my Las Vegas home for which a countdown has already started. As you know that I did not come to the University of Nizwa (UN) just to teach 50% more of my teaching load at UNLV (University of Nevada Las Vegas) for < 50 % of my salary. My objective was to have a taste of cultural and academic life of Middle East, which Oman has provided me. I have already found this experience very enriching, since nearly fifty *Reflections* have been written! All of you are a big part of it.

This *Reflective* note is triggered by instances of open cheating during the last weekly quiz. A couple of you flaunted my instructions. It has **two** serious consequences. **Number One**; if you are so daring about cheating in the last year of your college life, then it means it has been a part of the UN culture since the very first year. Think of your responsibilities as the first graduating class of the UN. What kind leadership you will provide later on in life, if cheating is deeply set in the foundation of your college degree?

Academic cheating is a law and order problem in the nearby Indian subcontinent, where I come from. It may be due to historic illiteracy, tough competitions and scarcity of jobs there. But, no one has gone to the top of a profession by cheating alone. One has to be original at some point in time. I hope you bear it in mind.

For the Omanis, there is no reason to cheat, as the jobs are almost guaranteed, if you want to work. The government jobs are secured. Also, under a policy of Omanization, the private companies have to hire and retain a certain percentage of Omanis. If you are competent, then it is great. If you are not competent, then your salary will be an additional tax on the company.

Number Two; over the last 13 weeks, a constant theme of my instruction has been to turn you into thinking persons. There are signs of breakthrough in a few cases. However, a prerequisite to deductive thinking is your devotion to mathematics, measured by your attendance, class participation and homework. In this respect, not even a single student has maintained a perfect attendance! Conservatively speaking, **60% of you have missed 60% of the classes**. It does not work in the learning of mathematics.

Involving you in class participation has been a challenge. Most of you sit out with folded arms, as if a watching a movie. There is no studying during the weekends and little after the classes on the same day. Home work is done minimally. I had to tell one student that what you have done in six weeks, I used to do more than it in one day before an exam.

Well, aside mathematical aspects, I have been very pleased with your grace, modesty, and manners. It is all a part of the culture of the land, and freedom enjoyed by the Omanis for centuries. I will cherish the memories of my association with you. All the best!

May 03, 2009 (Oman)

BROCCOLIS, CARROTS & MATH

"Read these chapters with the mindset of younger days, when forced by parents, you reluctantly nibbled on carrots, broccoli and celery." Yesterday, I told it to my students in *Survey of Mathematical Problems II* (MAT 712). It is a required course in the **Teaching Concentration** for an MS degree. The choice of topics is a function of students' curiosity and instructor's expertise. Thus, there is a lot of room for innovation in teaching this course. I always look forward to such an opportunity. The upper division seminars in the UNLV's Honors College also provide such a platform.

Two years ago, I taught this course for the first time. It was on a short notice, and I chose John Stillwell's, *Mathematics and its History*. Partly due to the fact that the American students are conditioned to having textbooks in every course, I did library and online searches for a suitable textbook. Also, given any topic under the sun, in the USA today, a book exists on it. It sounds like a typical existence theorem, for which math is known. This book has been used for Part I (MAT 711) too, as there is enough material for a year. This term, I had ample time to look for a 'better' textbook, but this book pulled me again, as if asking for one more shot. Finding an alternative textbook is an assignment for the students knowing digital resources. Let us see, how Stillwell's luck turns out next.

The title of the book is a bit misleading. It has little semblance with typical math history books that begin with Egyptian and Babylonian mathematics, and so on. The biographical notes are placed at the end of each chapter. The chapters are sprinkled with solid mathematics topics. For instances, it discusses rational triangles, regular polyhedra, transcendental numbers/functions, algebraic numbers/curves/functions, genus of curves, elliptic integrals/functions/curves, corner stone in the proof of *Fermat's Last Theorem*. Though I pride in my mathematical diversity and generality, still, I encountered new themes beautifully braided in this book. Stillwell is to be applauded for this book, as mathematicians often think of a textbook that covers all essential topics in a mathematically holistic manner.

In all traditional courses, **one can never learn math by reading math textbooks alone**. One must squat on the floor, or sit at the edge of chair for doing mathematics. But this course is truly exceptional. The chapters run on tracks that sometimes run parallel and sometimes orthogonal to the topics covered from the handouts. It requires organization. The challenge is met, as the students are mature and make connections with their mathematical goals.

Also, what is the importance of the study of original works of great mathematicians? Most undergraduate students study Shakespeare and Greek classics in literature, philosophy, and history. The music students study and play the compositions of great masters; true in other fine art areas too. It is not uncommon in social sciences to go after the original sources. However, in sciences, due to over specialization, the students and faculty alike may struggle in comprehending the great works like that of Gauss, Euler and Cauchy, to name a few legends. The purpose of instruction is also to awe and inspire the students by exposing them to the great minds, as one feels, say, while standing before Egyptian pyramids. At the next meeting, I will show *Principia Mathematica*, the 3-volume magnum opus of Russell and Whitehead, undertaken in 1900, and finished in 1913.

Oct 22, 2009

COMMENTS

I ran across math and its history about a couple of years ago. I saw it in a book catalog (Sapnaonline in India) and with our exchange rate, it was cheap (only problem is to get someone to bring it with them to the U.S.). I found it to be a precious book with real stuff to digest, and so it sat on my shelf for occasional nibbles. Later, around last year, I found out that he has authored many books, and on browsing thru them, found his writing style quite suited to my level and self-study. At present, I am trying to learn what I can from his '4 pillars of geometry'. All this is the initial steps in the long long road to understanding tensors, Riemannian geometry, General relativity. ....
Regards. **RAJA**

EQUIVALENCING: DANCES & PROOFS

1. The *Webster* defines 'Choreography' as: the art of symbolically representing dancing; the composition; arrangement of dances especially for ballet.
2. Lately, I have even watched dances that are mathematically choreographed. There are patterns described by mathematical functions/graphs and algebraic structures like groups, which are dynamically transformed as dance routines. One such composition was presented a couple of years ago at an annual Joint Mathematics Meeting (JMM).
3. After decades of watching dance performers both eastern and western, I am beginning to see similarities between mathematics, as art; and dance, as structures.

4. Through mathematics, we better understand human problems, when its mathematical model is solved. With a medium of dance, the choreographer evokes human emotions and appreciation of a slice of life pertaining to the present, past, or even future.

5. Currently, I am teaching a first course on proofs in mathematics. In simple jargon, a mathematical proof of statement is a sequence of steps (not necessarily unique) that begin with some axioms, postulates and previous proofs that result in the deduction of a given statement.

6. A single dance performance is like a single mathematics problem.

7. Math students, drilling on scores of similar problems, may be akin to the dancers practicing on the movements of different limbs along with facial expressions in order to generate a particular mood in the audience. However, a math problem solver is not at all concerned about the mood of his/her 'audience" (often none). Mathematics has no element of showmanship.

8. A dance performance lasting 60-90 minutes may have one or two themes achieved in one or two groups of dances. Often, a good math theorem contains smaller theorems and corollaries.

9. There is a contrast. Math students study old proofs for learning techniques, but reproducing an old proof earns no credits. In dancing, it is common for a performance running for several days – a test of its popularity.

Some Questions At Large:

(a) What kind of mathematical knowledge can be integrated in dance choreography?

(b) Can math be applied in dancing, as math has in-roaded music, finance, investments besides traditional social and natural sciences, and engineering? The abstracts (#749, 2010) of two papers, presented at the JMM in Jan 2010, provide lively examples.

(c) Conversely, does a particular dance genre help in the learning of some mathematics that I could tell my students that go and take this dance course (apart from Dance Appreciation/101). Can anyone benefit from dancing beyond physical fitness out of dancing as a total exercise?

(d) All this is still at gross levels. The deeper question is at the subconscious levels - how creatively choreographers and mathematicians think - one for a new composition, and the other for a new proof. One may be working in a dance studio and the other sitting in an office - while symbols are swirling in their minds.

(e) The highlights are when the symbols fly out in formations. One set of symbols may burst out into a dance form, and the other as proof of a theorem – call it a dance of mathematical symbols. Relatively speaking, one has larger visual appeal than of the other.

(f) My curiosity remains of internalized states of mind and the possibility of a bridge over them.

Feb 01, 2010

COMMENTS

Hi Satish, Thanks for sending this extensive set of thoughts about math and dance. You raise many interesting points and questions. I don't have time to address many of the points at the moment. You might like to take a look at our *Math Dance* book, by Erik Stern, Scott Kim, and myself, address for purchase and other info available through our web site, http://www.mathdance.org. That book is mostly designed for K-12 teachers wanting to make connections in the classroom.

I'm guessing the composition you saw at JMM was part of a presentation Sarah-Marie Belcastro and I did at the San Diego conference two years ago. Having been involved in bridging and connecting dance and mathematics for over 20 years, I would say that the connections and possibilities for connections are many and varied. I have often observed that the way mathematicians talk about a particular mathematics talk or presentation is remarkably similar to how dancers discuss particular performances.

Creative work in the arts and sciences seem to me to show many parallels; many people have written about this. See for example, the book Art Science: http://www.hup.harvard.edu/catalog/EDWART.html

Or Beveridge's *The Art of Scientific Investigation*:

http://www.amazon.com/Art-Scientific-Investigation-William-Beveridge/dp/0394701291

(This book was used as the text for a dance composition class I took taught by well-known dancer/teacher Daniel Nagrin, over 30 years ago.

Or the even earlier writings of Arthur Koestler, such as INSIGHT AND OUTLOOK AN INQUIRY INTO THE COMMON FOUNDATIONS OF SCIENCE, ART AND SOCIAL ETHICS

http://www.questia.com/library/literature/fiction/arthur-koestler.jsp

Sorry I cannot respond further at the moment, but thank you for sending these thoughts. I hope you pursue the questions you raise! I'll forward this to Erik Stern, as he may have further thoughts.

Karl Schaffer

CAPSTONING CALCULUS

Calculus is the most stimulating course for any instructor to teach and students to learn. Nevertheless, this statement does not pass any judgment on the usefulness of calculus-based mathematics over precalculus or finite mathematics. The main reason is that calculus gives human mind some dizzy flights of imagination, intuition and rationalism - all in the notion of infinity. For those not exposed to mathematics, infinity is just a dictionary word - capturing non-finiteness. In the study of set theory and transfinite numbers, infinity means infinitely many infinities!

Don't we all want to feel high at times? It is a sign of creativity! Studying mathematics means being drug free in a traditional sense. Yes, one cannot do conventional research in mathematics under the influence of mind-altering drugs. However, people are known to have composed great songs, created great music, did master paintings, and produced psychedelic arts in the grips of chemical substances.

I am always carried away while introducing the concept of Limit. Mathematical concept of Limit is ultimate in human intellectual endeavors. Newton understood it so well that through his infinitesimals, he derived a dozen principles/laws in mechanics, heat and light! The ε- δ definition of Limit is elegant. Paradoxically, it is useless in deciding a question of existence or non-existence of the Limit of an arbitrary function at a point. Life is full of such scenarios!

Last week, while introducing Limit of vector-valued functions in a 5-week Calculus III course, it occurred to me that every student must write a 500-word calculus report soon after it. After all, it is only by speaking and writing on/about a topic that its in-depth understanding sets in. I immediately put myself in students' place and traveled back in time in India of the 1950s. I recalled my frustration in applying Limit definition in solving problems. There being no pop quizzes or tests, one could afford to take a long time to figure the difficulties out before the final comprehensive exam given at the end of the year.

During my college days (1955-59), apart from some proofs, the main emphasis was on solving exotic problems. The two instructors taught a total of 9-11 math courses during the last two years of Honors in Mathematics - entirely different from any US college honor system. Their personalities, instructional styles and teaching philosophies were poles apart. Those images still reel out of my mind.

A word must be said about textbooks used in India of my era. The 'hard' cover books lasted only a month. Bookbinding reflects the technological advancements of a nation. India had won its freedom only eight years before I started my calculus journey. The textbooks were smaller and lesser in pages. They had one or two examples, as compared with current US textbooks filling half the pages with examples. Some textbooks had answers at the end. The entire system of education was British colonial – however, far different from what was prevalent in the British Isles.

I want students to recollect on anything connected with calculus. My underlying belief is that calculus reaches out to every gamut of human thought. I am confident that the collection of these reports will be a unique kaleidoscope of calculus. I look forward to reading them. Apart from teaching the new students, not much refreshing is there for an instructor who has been in business for 40+ years.

July 18, 2010/July, 2014

INTEGRITY OF SUMMER COURSES

For the last couple of summers, the number of students, taking two mathematics courses during five-week sessions, has been on the rise. Partly, it may be due to high unemployment in Nevada that people come back to schools to re-train themselves in new areas. Naturally, they want to quickly finish the courses and get back to work. It is also good for the university for the money it brings in - particularly, during tight financial conditions. This overload of two courses hits the students at the end of the first or second week when the work starts piling up. Every Friday, I remind the students that there is no weekend during a summer session!

For instance, several students are taking **Discrete Mathematics I** (MATH 251), the first proof course and **Linear algebra** (MATH 330), both abstract and applied courses. After attending the classes, they are left with little time for homework. In a math course, every hour in-class requires at least two hours outside. On the top, most students miss a lecture or two for varied reasons. It becomes a bit frustrating for an instructor when new material is being covered, but some students are hung up with old one. While covering the syllabus, it is a constant battle between lowering your benchmarks and raising students' bars.

Last week, I frankly told the students that there are three aspects of this overload. The Number one is your attitude towards the courses. Are you trivializing learning? Are your course expectations so low that the lowest passing grade, D Minus, would satisfy you? Some departments do accept any passing grade in math courses for their majors. Repeating courses is no longer an academic stigma. Rather, it is a reflection of shifting moral norms in the society. UNLV students are very frank and realistic about it, as they often shuffle studies between fixed points of their families and jobs. During my college days in India, students were full time – like 'professional' students – by and large, no jobs and families.

The second aspect is students' perspective of instructors. "I am doing great in the other math course; it is in your course that I am having problems." It does not take much to find out about the other course.

The entire instruction and exams are watered down, and made easier with inflated grades. This scenario is common. There are always some instructors who would give 90% of the grades in As and Bs. There is literally nothing that can be done about it. It is academic freedom in self-governance of the US higher education. Above all, the present environment is getting litigious.

However, I appeal to the third aspect - the image of Mathematics Department in particular, and of UNLV in general. There is a large number of local students who study out-of-state, but take summer courses while visiting parents. UNLV math courses are now transferrable. It would bother me, if such a student boasts about finishing two math courses, say, *Calculus III* and *Linear Algebra,* during a five-week session. It would reflect on UNLV's academic standards.

Institutional image is very important in both academics and athletics. Once, it is brought down or tarnished, it takes long time to re-build it. Good image of a department is beneficial for everyone. **Faculty advising undergraduate majors can only make a difference**, though it is only recommendatory. Unfortunately, academic advising by faculty has become a relic of university life, since it has been shifted to the college advising centers.

July 26, 2010/July, 2014

COMMENTS

I enjoyed reading this reflection, Dr Bhatnagar. Just wanted to double check what you wrote about the minimum passing grade. I understand that the minimum passing grade is a C, with C- and below being failing grades. Is this correct? Cheers, **Matt**

2.   Your reflections always awe me. Thank you. **Rohani**

I wrote: Glad to hear! Are you awed with my ideas, styles, or combination of things? Yes, they come from the kernel of my experience and wrapped in passionate expressions.

Rohani: I think both... especially your last paragraph. I shared your writing to a bunch of Malaysian postgraduates here, who are mostly academicians... I'll let you know if any of them responded to it. Regards.

3.   Satish, The summer, linear algebra class that I taught is legendary. The students I meet from that class still remember it. They were good, hardworking and I enjoyed that class. At the end of the 2nd week, I jumped ahead and started the abstract part of the course so they would have more time to absorb material. We continued the computational part and the algebra together . What's missing in that course and nearly all others in teaching is the follow up study. Where are those students in life and what are they doing? **PA**

4.   Hi, my name is Anna Starks. I am currently a PTI-GA in the math dept. I normally just read your comments and mostly agree with you. I have been a high school math teacher for eight years before coming back to school for my masters. I was very confused in the beginning when I started teaching college and found most of my students complaining that my class was either tough or the material too difficult. However, by the time I was done with my first group I had only one F out of 100 students. I'm not by any means an easy teacher and my exams are hard (according to several professors who have looked at them).

However, I am a trained teacher and I know how to put together a lesson plan that flows well and works with the most diverse amount of students. That has always been my strong suit according to every principal I have taught under. My students always did better on state tests then my colleagues. I am currently holding a teaching license in both Nevada and Wisconsin.

Now when you talk about image of this school and dept, according to my students thus far, it is not good. Some of my students have taken the same class three times, not for lack of trying, but for the lack of the instructors understanding of last minute planning equals bad learning experience. Sadly, as a GA, I can do nothing about this but make my class the best I can. However, most of the GAs have no training so they teach the way they learn. Which is wrong, as any good teacher knows. A teacher needs to be as flexible as possible in order to get the material across. Now, I am not sure if the dept could do anything to help with the actual GAs learning how to do lessons but it might help with the overall reputation of the math dept. I would even be willing to help out with a mini-lesson on it.

Although this goes far from your worry about the students taking too many courses during the summer in one session. I agree this year I had several students taking four courses in one session! I am not sure how that happens and makes me worried that they aren't actually retaining anything after the courses are done. Thanks, *Anna Starks*

A 4-DIMENSIONAL CALISTHENIC

The subject of 4-space dimensions is very natural, yet intriguing – always drawing the curious young and pros alike. It, perhaps, stems from an innate human desire to break away from the 'shackles' of 3- space dimensional life. Science-fiction writers thrive on it, but not as much as they do in time travels – diving back in time and leaping into future. Mathematicians are really cool about the fourth dimension of distance. For instance, they have been studying R^n, n-dimensional Euclidean space for ages - irrespective of its physical interpretations.

Nevertheless, human flights of imagination want to 'experience' the four-dimensional world sitting out somewhere in a 'super cosmos'. At least, its beginning can be pinpointed with the study of plane analytic geometry. Using the Cartesian coordinates, named after Rene Descartes (1596-1650), the unique representation of a point in a coordinate plane can be understood by a 12-year old kid today. Incidentally, this representation is one of the ten great moments in the history of mathematics - according to Howard Eaves (1911- 2004), a doyen of modern history of mathematics.

My curiosity about the four-space dimensional (4-D) universe was first whetted during the 1950s, when I 'heard' that Einstein's General Theory of Relativity explains four-dimensional world. I studied it for a year after my master's, which was essentially in mathematical physics. A physicist friend, at UNLV, regularly teaches a course on Special Theory of Relativity that is within the reach of college freshmen. Eventually, I realized that Einstein's fourth dimension was not of all space, but of time too. Corresponding to Euclidean point in space, Einstein defined an Event as - three space coordinates and the fourth one of time. I think, Einstein's understanding of three-dimension world was deeper, whereas that of Newton was wide and practical.

This train of thought was re-stirred yesterday, while reading through a weekly project report of a student in my graduate course, *Survey of Mathematical Problems I* (MAT 711), where independent library research is encouraged beyond the class material. She has been studying a book, *50 Mathematical Ideas You Really Need To Know* (by Tony Crilly). Naturally, her mind, like that of zillions before, was boggled by the fourth space dimension. To top it off, she inserted a 2-dimensional diagram of a 4-dimenstional cube! That really turned me on its exploration.

Here is an approach to a sectional understanding of a 4-dimensional cube. For the sake of unifying nomenclature, let us start from a 'cube' in 1-D – it is a line segment of one unit in length. Its boundary (assuming boundary of dimension one less) consists two Euclidean points/'vertices' (defined of dimension zero). Next, take a 'cube' in 2-D – it is our friendly square in a plane. It has four vertices and the boundary consists of four 1-D line segments. So far, so good. Moving on to a familiar cube in 3-D, it has eight vertices, six 2-D boundary faces and twelve 1-D edges. Let it be reminded that the boundary of a 'cube' in any dimension is one less than that of a cube.

Therefore, the challenge becomes in 'visualizing' the 3-D boundary of a 4-D cube. From the 'pattern', this boundary consists of 3-D cubes! Yes. How many 3-D cubes make the boundary of a 4-D cube? It is eight. Visualize eight 3-D cubes snuggled all around together making the 'exterior' of a 4-D 'interior space'. I cannot 'see' it, but mathematics tells it so. Moreover, it has sixteen 0-D vertices, ninety-six 1-D edges, and forty-eight 2-D 'faces'.

Once in a while, one must feel 'high' by stretching the limits of one's body, mind, or soul - each having infinitely many arenas! If anyone wants to play more with a 4-D cube, then find the number of its diagonals, defined as, 1-D line segments, joining two points not in the same 2-D face. Or, how about a 4-D formula corresponding to the Euler Formula for 3-D convex polyhedrons, namely, F (for number of faces) + V (for vertices) = E (for edges) + 2? It must be known to someone, or posted on a website.

Once human intellect is empowered with the deductiveness of mathematical thinking, then nothing is intimidating – though it may not be always easy.

Oct 30, 2010

COMMENTS

Thank you for the reflection. It was indeed an interesting read. **Matt**

Good! **Angel Muleshkov,** math professor at UNLV

PERSONAL REMARKS

INTEGRATION LIES IN INTEGRATION

Integration problems of calculus have held all-time fascination for me. It was 50+ years ago that I was first hooked on them. The power of integration reached new heights while studying classical mechanics, electricity & magnetism and hydromechanics during both for my bachelor's and master's from Panjab University, Chandigarh. Once those physics problems are set up mathematically, it is all about solving differential equations and evaluating esoteric integrals. Naturally, it has built my deeper appreciation for applications and beauty of integral calculus – far beyond its historical reasons.

Of course, it all started in India, where college education was for a few selective and privileged students. There is no comparison, say, with present UNLV students. In India of the 1950s, we were really 'professional' students in the sense that we had no other obligations besides studying. One granddaddy-final examination system has no resemblance with the US system of continuous evaluation. Consequently, in India, the students and instructors would hunt for challenging problems, beyond their textbooks, in order to prepare for the Final. In a way, the Final exam also tested the instructors - how well they had prepared their students.

Well, these thought were triggered off yesterday, as I finished devoting two 150-minute periods in discussing integration problems in a graduate course, MAT 712 (*Survey of Mathematical Problems II*). The two-semester sequence, MAT 711-712, is exclusively designed and required for students in the *Teaching Concentration* - one of the four concentrations for MS in mathematics at UNLV. Out of six students enrolled in this course, three are full-time math teachers in high schools, and the remaining three would be similarly placed in near future.

There is underlying emphasis on topics in the sense that "*connections (be) made between the mathematical content of this course and mathematical content for secondary education*". This open-endedness description makes the course organization challenging. The foremost consideration in running this course is that there must be a solid common intersection between the interests of the instructor and that of students, who have the most diverse mathematical backgrounds. My approach and objectives are to prepare these students so that they can confidently face any group of high school mathematics students - including AP (Advance Placement), IB (International Baccalaureate), Honors, or any accelerated course work.

To my dismay and surprise, integration problems, in a popular *Calculus* textbook by James Stewart, currently adopted at UNLV, are relatively jokes. It was disappointing to note the deletion of sections of challenging problems included in earlier editions – call it, dumbing down of calculus. Searching over the recent issues of the *College Mathematics Journal* produced only one problem:

Evaluate, $\int_0^1 \left(\left(1 - x^a\right)^{\frac{1}{a}} - x \right)^2 dx$, *for a*>0. (Quickie # 1008, CMJ, Feb, 2011)

Involving the students in the search of challenging integration problems produced interesting findings. It impressed me just how much we are living in the internet age. However, ninety percent of the online integral problems are trivial – catering to the lowest common denominator! One student found a bunch of six exotic problems. Here is one of them discussed in the class: Evaluate, $\int \sin(101x)(\sin x)^{99} dx$ (from MIT Integration Bee)

The MIT integration bee reminds me of an incidence that happened to me 20+ years ago, when the first symbolic integration was done by computer software. A former colleague, Tom Schaffter, who was also the most enthusiastic user of technology in math courses, 'set me up against the computer'. I won it then! Nevertheless, like the present chess softwares, integration softwares must have become a lot 'smarter', whereas, my skills have been rusting for lack of regular challenges. A few years ago, I was delighted to read that Penn State Math Dept was holding an undergraduate competition on integration problems. However, I did not find any current information on it from their website.

While battling with integration problems, I observed a contrasting feature between differentiation and integration. Historically, both started with equally challenging geometric problems. Nevertheless, I tell my calculus students that any differentiation problem can be done essentially in one line, but an integration problem may fill out a few sheets.

A hallmark of my instruction is encouraging students by giving extra credits for providing alternate solutions of a problem – whether on a quiz or test. Integration problems are perfect fit for it, as some of them can be done by 4-6 different methods. It fits into my philosophy of life that there are different points of view of an issue or solutions of a human problem.

For instance, a disease has different treatments in different systems of medicine – like the western allopathy and homeopathy, naturopathy, Middle Eastern *Unaani*, Indian Ayurvedic, Chinese herbal and acupuncture, and many local indigenous systems. In the world of mathematics alone, there is no conflict between any two solutions of a problem. But, say, in the practice of medicine, one system constantly fights to drive the other out of business by reducing it to quackery.

In nutshell, like some holistic food for body, integration problems are holistic for the brain cells. It is fun to play with them at any time, age, or place. Let us propagate integration!

Feb 17, 2011

COMMENTS

Quite interesting remarks. There is the unfortunate idea that all the techniques of integration that we learned have been rendered 'useless' by today's computers. So why memorize the multiplication table. I do get students who need the calculator for 6 x 7. Life changes. **RAJA**

Dear Professor Satish; I enjoyed very much with your article. It is wonderful, thank you. With best regards, yours sincerely**, Dr. Ahmed El-Karamany,** former, Head of Mathematics Department University of Nizwa, Nizwa, Sultanate of Oman

HOMEWORK PROPELS PERSONA

"He does his homework before a meeting and comes prepared." and "Time is wasted, if homework is not done." etc. are some of the popular phrases emphasizing the importance of homework in American way of life. Homework embodies attitudes, discipline and work ethics. Yes, it does originate from academic confines - starting from school days and doubling up in college. Irrespective of school or college, homework is far more pronounced in the study of mathematics than in any other discipline.

These thoughts floated into my mind today, as I was checking a pile of students' homeworks while they were taking the Test # 2 in a *Linear Algebra* (MATH 330) - a first 'abstract-ly' course. It is perfect utilization of instructor's class time when the students are being tested. In the US academe, instructor does not have to worry about students cheating the moment the eyes are off them. In Asian countries, it has become far more than a law and order problem.

Let me add a touch of history to math homework at UNLV. Early on through the 1980s, faculty members were assisted by graders. Ten years ago, the budget cuts gradually eliminated graders from all lower division courses (100-200 levels). From personal experiences, I encourage peer learning and small study groups. It is a non-issue, if two or three students even have identical solutions. Students are even free to discuss any homework problem with me. Thus, it is enough to check homework, every 3-4 weeks. It has been satisfying in all respects. However, during the last 4-5 years, the IT boom has brought a new paradigm shift in the domain of homework. There are all kinds of math tutorial websites that students can sign up free or with a lump fee.

The US students are used to a structure about homework problems. On Day #1, a list of problems is distributed - like, *Sec 3.2 (Section 2 of Chapter 3): exercises: 10-30*. It is explained that they are not traditional homework problems, in the sense, due on a certain day. Instead, these problems are for the sole purpose of smart reviewing before a test. Say, in this instance, there is no need to waste time in doing problems #1-9, as they become elementary after 2-3 weeks. Any problem after # 30 may not be relevant for test purposes. However, as far as homework is concerned, do all the problems unless they are specifically deleted. The notation, like, [17-20] means problems # 17 through # 20 are excluded for any class time, quiz or test. However, students are free to discuss any problem with me.

In a homework scenario presented today, out of 35 students, only 4 had done all the problems, say, from 1- 40, if the exercise set had 40 problems. Most of them started from # 10 and stopped at # 30 – some did the odd numbered only. It appears 2-3 generations have gone by believing that one can get by with minimal homework in academics. Mathematical concepts literally evaporate if not worked in every day. It seems that the drills and practice hours are witnessed in athletics alone. I often look up at my student athletes while stressing this point. Yes, the US stakes are higher in athletics.

My grading criteria are simple, as I watch for quantity and quality of problems. If a student has done 90 % of the textbook problems and has put them neatly together, then he/she may earn 10 points out of 10. My scoring is like scoring a round of boxing - rarely anyone gets less than 6.

Mar 21, 2011

INTEGRATING MATH COURSES IN ….!

People go to the restaurants for an hour and can talk for a long time about food and ambience; they go to the movies or ballgames for 2-3 hours and afterwards would discuss and dissect the events from different angles, and so on. However, when it comes to a math course studied for 16 weeks, one cannot speak about it even for two minutes! Students do share with each other something about a course taken in social studies, fine arts, humanities, and even in science and engineering. In this regard, mathematics is in a league of its own.

For the last few years, I have been encouraging my students to write an extra-credit report on finding/making any connections with topic(s) in math courses – not any summary of the topics or evaluation of instruction. The other connecting node could be anything in life - another course, a thought system, hobby, or job etc. It applies to math courses at any level – lower, upper, or graduate. The course contents are retained and recycled for any application, if at least, a part of it can be hinged with something tangible. Learning that is internalized lasts longer. Communication between two persons, flow of information between two points, any application, or bridge – they all are relationships between two shores – real or abstract.

A question is how to work the students on this exercise? It is a gentle process of humanizing math definitions, theorems and problems, at any given opportunity during the course of lectures. Its importance is periodically stressed. Moreover, by the end of the 10th week, having written two other extra credit reports, the students have already tasted some benefits of this non-traditional feature. **Writing reinforces points of learning**. Under no condition is this report accepted even an hour before the final exam. Yes, preparation for a comprehensive final exam is very important in the development of this thought process. For instance, this semester, the final exam was scheduled on Wednesday, and the reports were electronically due by the following Saturday – three days after.

I must admit, such a report is not always easy to write. In courses - like calculus and precalculus, even the sophomores are able it to relate with something. However, each report is looked at in a positive manner. It is a very small step in the direction of students' journey of intellectual exploration - like a seed being planted during springtime of their lives - that is most likely to sprout and bloom in future.

A word from an instructor's perspective is in order. How long and how much can an instructor remain excited about teaching a course? Monotonous teaching is a different ballgame. I still belong to the passionate class. For instance, I taught Math 330 (Linear Algebra) for the first time during Summer 1975, and have done it sixteen times since then. **Where is my stimulus money?** Such a report takes care of all the x-variables.

Personally, I can't wait to read these reports, as soon as they chime into my inbox. There is an element in each report that is hilarious, funny, unbelievable, boring, trivial, most unexpected, or creative - name any other adjective. It is enriching to read them all. Mathematicians are slow readers, but 200 words, +/- 5 words are within anyone's reading capacity in this Twitter age.

Linear Algebra is a different course. Its prerequisite is Calculus II - mainly for mathematical exposure, rather than, for any topical reasons. If I have to write 200 words on this course, then apart from exposure to newer mathematical thinking generated by concepts – like, linear transformations and vector spaces, it is challenging to relate the material with anything tangible. **But I tangentially mention the US Senators and HR in the context of linearly independent vectors and bases of a vector space**. Matrices and row reductions are definitely popular with students' previous high school math background and present courses. Here are one line extracts from some reports:

"..relating with ME 319/MATLAB", "reduce matrices…..the game Sudoku", "Differential equations. …….Prior to taking this class I only knew how to find the det of 2x2 matrices", "…reminded me my past computer classes..", "..applications in my personal life, particularly with programming..", "Math 283….. it has made my business (tutoring) easier. Joking concerning whether or not 5th floor of the residence hall was a subspace." or not. We went through the three rules of subspace", "3-D animation, matrices and movie Thor…", "Video games and three dimensional matrices..", "vectors, matrices and robotics", "After this course, I couldn't believe how trivial the solutions to my problem of (of video games) were.", "Linear Algebra has firm set of rules which are well defined and understood.", "….related with Math 251 being taken in parallel", "Related it with secondary education math as major.", "From the internet learnt about the applications of linear algebra and that motivated for studying.", "… However, this course has interested me to continue taking higher level math classes and I might even end up minoring in Math.", "This course is more thinking abstractly. I was humbled by this class."

These reports remain posted outside my office for a month. I like to display 'my little world of mathematics' for students, visitors and guests who may be walking through the hallways. Actually, once a while, I do walk by the faculty offices in different departments and colleges. Reading notes, signs, clips, cartoons, comic strips, pictures, flyers and posters are quite amusing and informational. Relatively speaking, the notice boards and office doors of the math faculty are least enchanting. The departments of Kinesiology, Psychology and Art top the list for interesting stuff – including xxx – in the name of academic freedom!

Finally, in all, 25 out of 37 students submitted these reports, though they were not mandatory. The class GPA is 2.13 - reflecting students' general struggle with this material. Nearly 15 % were repeaters. The course begins with row reductions and matrices, a down-to-earth approach, as compared with the extreme approach - starting with abstract vector spaces. Nevertheless, those who wrote such an extra-credit report will never forget a total course experience.

May 22, 2011

COMMENTS

Very enjoyable! I was informed of some research on math performance--where those taking an exam did significantly better when starting with easy and proceeding to hard (as compared to hard, then easy). I think building confidence (without sacrificing content and academic rigour) is important and easier said than done! Good idea with how you started the course. **Aaron Harris**

Satish- Thank you for the Mathematical Reflections: 190. I always like to read about the great world of mathematics, and the wonderful things that can be done with it. As an example, in a course in mineralogy, as an assignment, I made a stereographic projection of the upper half of a pentagonal dodecahedron. The highest form of mathematics used was solid trigonometry, which involved plotting points in an X, Y & Z space. This is an example of how simple trig can be used to form complicated geometries.

George Washington, known as the father of this country, was a surveyor by trade. Surveying is an application of basic trig. Washington ended up leading the revolutionary army against the British, and became the first president of the country. So one may conclude that great things can be done from simply knowing basic mathematics. Keep up the great work. Jim

JUMP & HEAD START!

It is time to think about the course starting within a week. Please use full name and Rebelmail in any communication. This e-mail is not meant to distract you from a course currently being taken, or from any vacation, or work. The five-week summer courses are very intense. This course is lower division (100-200 levels), yet quite a few seniors are always there - but rarely, a freshman.

What is the point of this e-mail? It is basically to encourage you for getting a head start before the first class. It is a good to develop this attitude in life. Head start means that you buy the textbook a few days in advance of the starting date. Do bring it to the classes, as all problems are taken out of it. It is well written. Remember one thing about the textbooks - no author writes a textbook for only one school. As a matter of fact, the US textbooks are adopted all over the world. I saw them adopted when I taught in India, Malaysia and Oman. It is thus essential to skip some problems and material in order to customize it for the UNLV students.

Head start means a little more than a having a book. Putting it in straight words - never walk in cold in a class - much less of a math course. Find time to glance over new class material. During a session, after a class is over, while walking back to your car park or another class, bring into focus what you have enjoyed during a lecture and where you were totally lost. Play this mental game soon after every class. Its result will surprise you, and it may change your life.

The first day of classes is very important, particularly when a course meets for all the five days. It is like soup that lays the digestive foundation for the next courses of a gourmet meal. Take time to read the Preface of the book - pay special attention to the portion meant for the students. During the course, give one reading to the entire textbook, as if it is a part of ENG 101 course. Often, textbook reading is omitted, as the focus remains on examples and exercises. It is no less important to know the course instructor. Personally, I can recall all math instructors from high school to college to universities! Generally, confidence in the instructor breeds enthusiasm for the course. Also, browse over the introductory pages of the first chapter.

Talking of the first day, it is a measure of quality of instruction. Actually, it sets the US apart from rest of the world! During Spring-2009, I taught in the University of Nizwa, Oman - patterned after a university of Wisconsin campus. Any comparison stops here. Even a month before the start of the semester, the date of the first day of instruction was up in the air! The textbooks were delivered to my office and I was supposed to keep a record of issuing them to the students. It was after three weeks that 'real' instruction began. In that part of the world the textbooks are not bought from a bookstore or treasured after the course is over. The textbooks are collected back on the day of the Final exam.

Well, you would occasionally hear such mathematical stories - accumulated after fifty years of my college teaching. Yes, it was started in July, 1961 in Government Rajindra College, Bathinda, my hometown in India! Since 1974, Las Vegas has been my home in the US when I joined UNLV after PhD from Indiana University, Bloomington. Talking of stories, some of them are included in my first book, *Scattered Matherticles*; *Mathematical Reflections*, Volume 1 (2010). There is a nugget for everyone, whether one has any math background or not. It is not a supplementary book to the textbook, but will surely broaden your humanistic horizons of mathematics.

July 04, 2011/July, 2014

THE IMP OF PROOF IN MATH

"I understand mathematics, but I just can't do the proofs." That is how the authors of a textbook, *A Transition to Advanced Mathematics*, open up the Preface of its 7th edition. It has similar remarks spread over in the body – somewhat projecting that writing of proofs is mysteriously difficult, or a big deal - to say the least. Though I have used earlier editions of this textbook, this time, I felt that such remarks are fear mongering and confidence shaking for the students. Some students, by a word of mouth or from a previous failed attempt, are already apprehensive about proofs. Hence, such statements by the authors and instructors are not going to be helpful. At UNLV, the first four chapters of this textbook are generally covered in MATH 251 (*Discrete Mathematics I*), for which Calculus II is a co-requisite.

For the last couple of offerings, I have been taking an opposite approach of demystifying proof writing. It is pounded from Day #1 that each and every student, at this stage of mathematical exposure, has some innate understanding of what a proof is. This course provides a little structure and polish in their individual 'arts' of proving statements. Throughout the instruction, attempts are made to capitalize on students' prior knowledge of precalculus and calculus.

For instance, this year, on the very first day of a five-week summer session, I wrote down a popular proof problem from the scenario of integers (Section 4): **Prove that the sum of two even integers is even**. Of course, it was broadly mentioned what the definitions are and what properties of integers are assumed in this context. Apart from its proof, the ideas of verification and counterexamples were easily conveyed. Most students understood the essence of proof. To boost their confidence, I jumped to the last Section 7 of Chapter 1, and analyzed a proof of the problem: **Prove that if n is an integer and 3n + 1 is odd, then 2n + 8 is divisible by 4**. Of course, divisibility of integers was refreshed first.

It was on Day #2 that the propositional and predicate logic (Sections 1 and 2) were covered. However, another proof problem from Section 7 was taken up as continuation of confidence building process.

Of course, the excessive notations of logic (Section 3) are under-emphasized, as the probability of any one doing graduate work in mathematical logic is nearly zero. For instance, in this group of 16 students, there is only one math major, three from economics and finance, two fulltime high school math teachers, and the rest from computer science and different engineering areas. I believe textbook material has to be customized for the students in some sense.

Historically, ***Discrete Mathematic*** course is all-American, created in early 1980s. By the end of the 1970s, the proofs were literally banished from precalculus and calculus courses. This hysteria went to such an extreme that the IEEE published a calculus textbook for the engineering students. It did not have even a single definition and statement of a theorem! Naturally, the pendulum had to tilt eventually. Instead, gently re-integrating proofs in precalculus and calculus, as it was in pre-1950s era, a new 'proof' course was created. Incidentally, the demand for the proofs came from computer science! Math departments jumped at this opportunity and required it for their majors and minors too – followed by secondary math education majors. Its demand has been increasing ever since.

On a personal note, my exposure to the proofs started with the introduction of classical Euclidean Geometry of the plane. I was 14 and studying in the 10th grade in a high school in Bathinda (India). While I had mastered algebra with all its manipulative skills, and really appreciated its power in solving some real word problems, the proofs of the very first two propositions of Euclidean Geometry completely threw me off. My state of anger, confusion and surprise are still etched in my memory, as it went for nearly two weeks. However, equally vivid are the memories of the day of 'enlightenment' that came with the help of Ved Vyas Bagga, a classmate's older brother. I felt as if a foggy screen was suddenly removed from my mental eyes – like after a cataract surgery. I literally ran with Euclidean Geometry afterwards, and have loved it since then.

With over five decades of experience in the world of mathematics - as student and professional, I have come to a conclusion that there is nothing in the entire gamut of mathematics – a body of mathematics more intuitive, beautiful, elementary, simple, useful, complete, and analytical than plane Euclidean Geometry. Now, one can freely download all the books comprising ***Euclid's Elements*** and explore its time immemorial merits. According to math historian, Howard Eves, the two US presidents, Lincoln (1861-1865) and Garfield (1881) are known to have deeply studied Euclidean Geometry.

It is time to re-introduce Euclidean Geometry for eight weeks for the college bound high school juniors or seniors. The students would then appreciate dry axiomatic geometry presently taught for full year. Sadly, at the college level, there is little hope, as the tools of analytic geometry are considered more powerful. Moreover, a college geometry course (MATH 480/680) fills in some holes. However, I did offer a one-credit experimental course on Euclidean Geometry, ***Back to Euclid*** (Math 380X) during a three-week, mini term in Jan 1988.

Finally, for any professional mathematician, proving, studying, playing with mathematical statements becomes natural like breathing. During instruction of any course, it is nearly impossible to ignore and bypass all the proofs. Again, it comes to me from the college curriculum in India of the 1950s, when proofs were emphasized in nearly 40% of class instruction and examinations. Hence, I can't resist proving one or two simple statements in any math course that is taught. Of course, the students are not tested on those proofs, but their minds are seeded forever with the nature of proofs in mathematics.

July 27, 2011/July, 2014

PS: Imp is my favorite abbreviation for 'important'. It is an archaic word – also means a 'little devil'!

COMMENTS

The incredible, but true, demise/disappearance of proof from the math textbooks/instruction is a crime. I don't have to mention to you how proof is the soul of mathematics. I have been forced to make a living playing with a make believe skeleton!! In 1990 when I started teaching algebra in the math dept, they still included the chapter on mathematical induction. In a semester or two they decided it was too hard for the students. With its disappearance, proof disappeared from all the subjects at the community college level. My one student, who wanted to major in physics, got totally lost when he transferred to a 4-yr and enrolled in 'a course in vector spaces'. In fact he had a nervous breakdown!! It is a tragedy too deep for tears. **RAJA**

PERSONAL REMARKS

PAYING FOR MATH HOMEWORK

[The following handout to the students was circulated when a media report made local headlines that math students were paying for having their homework done. It is not a new thing. Mathematics is universally difficult relatively. In every age and land, there are individual tutors and coaching organizations helping students in math on payment basis. In humanities, term papers have been openly sold for decades. However, the way it became a topic of campus conversation for a week, I decided to gauge its level with my students.]

Dear Calculus III Students,

I want your honest feedback on this media report in the making. Have you ever paid any one online/offline for getting your homework done in Calculus III, or in some other course? Personally, I do encourage small study groups even during class quizzes. The idea is that you can learn no leas from your peers. Besides, we discuss problems in the class and you are tested on textbook examples too. A difference that you may have noticed in my instruction is that I hold you responsible for all the problems - unless specifically deleted.

Homework carries at most 10 % of the weightage in lower division courses. For a number of reasons, I don't see any point in verifying the integrity of my students' efforts in homework they turned it in. My main point is that if a student pays someone to have his/her homework done, then it would show up in the performance of ten quizzes and 3-4 hourly tests. Above all, if one wants a minimum grade of C, then even if one gets all the 10% in homework, he/she has to be getting at least D+ on tests and quizzes for earning a C grade in the course. Most students don't do this simple math, no wonder - nearly 66% end up repeating Calculus III during summer session.

Your comments, in the space below, may help future students taking this course. You need not disclose your name or any other information. Thanks.

Aug 10, 2011

[Based on the response received, there was no evidence that my students pay for homework; a few rather strongly believe it is not the right way to learn math. Students in Calculus III are mostly junior and they understand that there is no short cut to learning mathematics except doing it with your own hands and brain. The bottom line is that one may have sex enjoyment by paying to a prostitute, but one cannot have joy of learning math by paying a tutor do the problems for you!]

PROMOTING MATHEMATICAL WRITING

Last week, a student wrote in his semester-ending final weekly report that he would be missing doing the weekly writing assignments. Being a 'mathematical' writer, I felt like having hit a home run! I have been encouraging free style writing in all mathematics courses taught during the last 15-20 years. However, **History of Mathematics** (MAT 714) course involves a lot of reading, class discussion, and library and online researches – so, a weekly report is essential here. Flowery language, creative phrases and reflective styles are promoted and applauded. Since the publication of my first volume of *Mathematical Reflections* last year, I have become more passionate about writing, in general.

Incidentally, I was not encouraged by anyone in my writing endeavor. On the contrary, I was discouraged by several persons - including my family members. However, I was convinced about getting deeper satisfaction, if writings continued irrespective of what the others may think of it. It is possible, if early on, one does not have to depend on royalty income from the writings. Here is snapshot evaluation of the writings of my four students who have finished this course. The objective is pure encouragement!

Andrzei's English has a streak of freshness about it. As a foreign student, like, once I was from India, he is from Poland. Being a competitive swimmer too, there is fluidity in his expression. Often, he coins good phrases and captures the essence of a topic. Also, it may be due to his artistic talent drawn from his love for mini TV productions. Apart from all this, he finds time to model for the artists. That frees him from some psychological inhibitions. A writer has to reveal his soul. Every reader looks for daringly new material.

Assia learnt English after moving to the US as a child. Her speech and writings do not betray the fact that English is her second language. Her weekly write-ups have been most comprehensive - displaying her control and confidence in writing. With a BS in engineering, as a graduate student, her vocabulary is sound. Often, people equally wonder at me - how a man of mathematics can write so extensively in

English. Assia may have a storehouse of stories to tell based upon her Afghani background. Her relatives may share their stories with her for putting them in black and white.

Maryann is a full time high school teacher. What that means is that she is professionally conditioned by all kinds of rules and regulations in the classroom and life. It is noticeable in her writings – in the choice of phrases, punctuation and structure of the sentences. However, like me, she also enjoys teaching in diverse places - like India and UK. That may eventually turn into a liberating factor. She has the potential of becoming an inspiring writer of mathematical stories - drawn from the classrooms of different cultures.

Amy is a full time teacher too. At times, I amusingly notice Mary and Amy conferring with each other, supposedly, on the English of my *Reflections*. It is looking at the usages like applying mathematical formulas. Amy's fear of oral presentation spells over into her verbal expression, and tightens her up. Getting over the oral part by joining a toastmasters club will help her get over the verbal too. On a personal note, in college, I was outspoken - thus, boldness entered into my writing. For instance, once I positively described a sex manual - when it came to writing an essay on a book that had influenced me most. I was 19 then - living in Bathinda, a puritanical and orthodox town in India.

Dec 01, 2011/July, 2014

COMMENTS

Tauji: Over the years you have covered a wide array of topics through your reflections, some controversial, others inspiring. Being raised in England, the education of young child has always been determined by the outcome of his/hers ability to demonstrate their analytical or creative aptitude. In my case, I had a thirst for Science and Mathematics and a reluctance to explore the English language, its importance and the rules that govern it. Due to a lack of mentorship and guidance, I forged ahead and became an analytical practitioner.

Today, I believe that children should be encouraged to explore the English language and its potential impact on their development. I would encourage educators to embrace your class (MAT 714) and introduce it at the elementary or junior high level, instead of introducing it at the postgraduate level. Of course, the material would be age appropriate but the education would bridge the gap between the children who exercise their right brains and those who exercise their left brains. It is something that I never understood or experimented with.

I do enjoy reading the reflections and it provides stimulating discussion with my colleagues.

Respectfully, **Madhu Gohil**

ON A RULE OF INTEGRATION

Most calculus textbooks in the US state and apply this product rule of integration in the following compact looking form,

$$\int u dv = uv - \int v du.$$ _____(1)

I call (1) the **differential form** of the Product Rule of Integration. However, one wonders - where are the **two** functions corresponding to the ones in the product form that are supposed to be integrated? That is where (1) is a bit fuzzy and **not** very functional.

Recall the **product rule differentiation** looks like:

$$\frac{d}{dx}[f(x)g(x)] = f(x)g'(x) + f'(x)g(x)$$ _____(*)

Here, one can clearly identify the two functions f and g in the product form.

By integrating both sides of (*), w.r.t. x, a corresponding form for integration of product is:

$$\int f(x)g'(x)dx = f(x)g(x) - \int f'(x)g(x)dx$$ _____(2)

By letting $G(x) = g'(x)$, (2) can be re-written as,

$$\int f(x)G(x)dx = f(x)[\int G(x)dx] - \int f'(x)$$

$$[\int G(x)dx]dx$$ _____(3)

On comparing (*) with (3), both the LHS are in the desirable product form, and the first terms on the RHS are in the same format. But the second term differ in sign, and so does the form of the second term. However, this form is far more functional than the differential form (1) or (2).

Remarks:

1. **Rule of Integration by Parts** won't work in general, if antiderivative/integral of at least one function is not known. For

example, $\int e^{(x^2)} \ln x \, dx$ is not easy for this rule, as anti-derivatives of e^{x^2}, or ln x are not standard.

2. For $\int e^x \ln x \, dx$, though we know the integral of e^x, still the rule does not work.

3. If you know the anti-derivatives of both, even then both may not yield a closed form of the integral. It is a good rule of integration, but not a mighty one! However, it has to be mastered any way.

March 08, 2012

[This is not a typical mathematical reflection, and yet it is included in this book. The reason being that every now and then, an instructor finds that by the middle of a semester, there is little collective learning going on in the class. Then, either he/she lets the course go down with students' gravity, or does soul searching in order to turn the group around. In this respect, athletic coaches are far more successful in motivating their teams - from a brink of defeat to a big time victory.]

OPEN LINE FRIDAY

The title is borrowed from the Friday format of Rush Limbaugh's radio talk show that has been airing since 1984. During the show's three-hour slot, his listeners are free to ask him any question. Well, it was triggered while grading Test # 3 (Math 283/Calculus III) during the Spring break of 2012. It was a lot of work, particularly keeping track of two 'versions' of the Test # 3, which were given to the students in order to understand the bottlenecks, grading your tests, and then making the final point adjustments for each problem. It was a lot of work.

Now that both the tests are back in your hands, I really want you to go deep into your mind, as to how you want to finish this course. How can I help you in this direction by changing any approach in my lecture presentation? Take up to 20 minutes to ponder over it, relate it with a math course where you have excelled, and tell me what is holding you back in this course.

Now four weeks of instruction and one week of exam are left. Assuming that the Spring break was mathematically productive, let us work together during this final stretch. You know me and I know you better than during the first two or three weeks. After each one of you has put down the individual analysis and suggestions, I would pool them together and see how it can be integrated with the Line and Surface Integrals of Chapter 13 – the epitome of Calculus III.

Yes, I would like you to put down your names, as that would help me to judge your progress from the Day # 1 to 21 to 31. Use the backside of this sheet to continue your commentary and analysis. I am convinced that this exercise would help you a long way in life.

April 09, 2012/May, 2014

PS: The net effect of this exercise was that the class performance did not decline further as the final comprehensive exam indicated.

ARCHING OVER CALCULUS III

Throughout a semester, I encourage my students to write with a flair for three extra credit reports. The third and last one is to be turned in after the final comprehensive exam is over. The purpose is to connect the material, thinking, concepts etc. learnt in the course with anything one is passionate about - be it another course, hobby, job, or activity. What follows below is a small sample of the write-ups from recent Calculus III students. Reading them is the most enjoyable part of the course. In order to avoid repetitions of thoughts and ideas, a gentle editing has been done:

".....There have also been very rewarding times like when I was awarded with the AFROTC scholarship. Through the good times and the bad, the ups and the downs of my experience in the end it is about **perseverance**. This relates to my experience in Calculus III because in calculus too, you must persevere........" **AFROTC experience**

"....I began to realize just how much calculus is involved in circuit theory. I had not really paid that much attention to it until I started looking for it. It was seemingly involved in all of the alternating current chapters....." **Circuit Theory**

"I would compare my experience and journey through calculus III to a true passion of mine that I have had to cut back on while in this class. Marathon running has become something that I have become very involved in over the last few years, and is very similar to this course. In ever marathon that I have ever run there are a few things that always happen and several moments of mind over matter.

"In the beginning of a race there is excitement about the location of the race, all the people that are around, getting a good start and having a final time as a goal and experiencing the challenge. This is just like the beginning of this course, I was excited and ready for the challenge. As you progress through a marathon there are little things that pop up along the way, maybe a shoelace comes untied, you have to readjust some article of clothing, or some other minor detail.

"Regardless you get to the first clock and see that you are at an okay time. This is like the first test in this course, it wasn't at the time that I wanted but it was still early so there was time to improve. As you continue in the marathon there may be a few other snags here and there, you might miss the aid station and not get the drink of water you were planning on a don't get the recovery food you needed but you make it to the half way point.

"In this course it was the second test, it is still not exactly where I want to be so as in a marathon you start to make adjustments to what you where previously doing. You might even scrap you original plan and start making scarifies on your goal time just so you can finish. As the marathon continues you get tired and become frustrated that all of your time spent training and all of the sacrifices you have made are now feeling like they were not enough, maybe you should have gotten in a longer run one weekend or gotten more sleep another night. These thoughts start creeping in anywhere between mile 18 and 22.

"This starts to occur after third test you begin to feel tired and have realized how much you have given up for this class but how there is still more that must be sacrificed in order to be successful. This feeling in a marathon continues and you must push through.

"Then you take the fourth test, sacrifice more and push through. I have to tell myself at this point in the marathon and this course to just keep moving, keep trying, shut-up and run, you can do this, it is a lot of internal talk to keep me motivated. You make it through the "wall" which every marathoner encounters. I think this is like taking the fourth test. You take the test and move on and try to prepare for the finish.

"The last 4 miles in a race are when you have to commit to finishing, and not just by walking but to finish strong and run in the final stretch. This is what the last week of this course was for me. There is so much riding on this last four miles (and this class). I had to focus only on this class and all of the information covered in it. I had to push through the pain and make the information stick. Hopefully the effort paid off. I am hoping that when I pass the finish line of calculus III I will see C:CC:CC as my final time.

"Finishing a marathon regardless of the time is a true accomplishment in and of itself. When you finish and get a time you were training for it is beyond amazing the feelings of joy and pride in achieving your goals. Even if you don't achieve the time you wanted you have learned a lot from your experience and take it with you in the next race. Regardless of whether or not I earned the grade that I needed for this course I have learned a lot and will take it with me in my future math courses." **Running Marathon**

"Well as I drive my little Subaru down these winding roads, my car could be a particle in space and the road, SR157, the line segment. I must be careful not to go to fast and find my tangent! As I drive my particle in space, down the mountain, with the mountains on my left and right with their sedimentary layers exposed layers, or exposing there gradients vectors. On my way down I see an airplane and wonder what the normal vector between "my particle" in space and the plane. Given the numbers I am sure I could figure it out. About half down I see a Metro truck on the way up and have some brief anxiety if my magnitude and direction is above the posted speed limit." **Mountain Driving**

"..... got tired and bored of school. So i became an alchemist, a tinkerer, somewhat of an inventor. I studied chemistry, rocketry, model jet engines, all kinds of odd little devices. But somehow it all got lost, as i proceeded to college i lost most of that curiosity. ..... It is until the last 2-3 weeks this MATH 283 class that felt i traveled in time. You asked us to think in how the course related to our life's and it got me thinking. .... I believe that it is unfortunate that it was until the end of the course that I was relating all to my daily life......... What i am most grateful for the course is perhaps that I am as I was as a child; curious and willing to learn the crazy ideas i once forgot.." **Math integral to life**

".......... Discovering how everything works is my passion in life. My math 283 class ties into most of the engineering classes I take. I use it every day in when I do my homework, and the equations help me visualize what is going on........... The semester before this one I took a physics 181 class, which focuses mainly on electricity and magnetism. Most of the equations used were integrals that were made very simple through symmetry. I didn't really understand what was going on when I calculated the flux of a surface or the current in a wire, but now that I took math 283 I understand exactly what was going on........... When people say "when am I ever going to use math after high school" I think to myself what a shame that they will never know calculus was used to make almost everything they use in their everyday lives." **Physics and Engineering**

".....One of the most important things that I learned was the proper use of tools and that it took

practice to properly utilize those tools. Through this course I came to understand that mathematics is an incredible and powerful tool. I also came to realize that mathematics should and will be the foundation of my engineering degree. Much of what I took away from the course became clearer near the end once I started practicing more and more. I started to see and understand the little nuggets of information and guidance that you gave throughout the semester. Like practicing enough that it becomes second nature or part of your DNA............ It's amazing that through mathematics many ideas or concepts can be years ahead of the technology to prove them........ Thank you for the enlightenment." **Mechanical Engineering**

"...As a civil engineering student and avid outdoorsman I often use surface contours when hiking or when grading a development site for future building and parking. These contours which I create or read while hiking are "Level Curves" as discussed within Chapter 11 of Calculus 3. These are just a few examples that have come to mind as ways math influences life and my passions are tied back to math fundamentals....." **Civil Engineering**

May, 2012

NAMES AND LEARNING

It was noon time, and I was driving to Mesquite, Nevada - 90 miles north of Las Vegas. Twenty miles earlier, I noticed a very huge billboard on the right side of Interstate 15 – amidst nothing else in the desert; total desolation. Unless the billboard is big enough, its message won't register on the motorists driving at 80 MPH. Any way, it only had the picture of a young beautiful girl and a message: ***Here, professors know me by my name!*** It was followed by a line: Southern Utah University, Cedar City, Utah, which is 150 miles North of Las Vegas. There is a sexy undertone in it, and sex sells everything! This billboard is placed to attract the Nevada students.

Being a professor and a reflective writer, this billboard really spun my thoughts in huge vortex. This semester, I have two classes one started with 27 students and the other with 57 students. Knowing the students by their names has been essential to my teaching style and philosophy. However, this time, I could not remember the names of all the 57 students. I was feeling disappointed. Is it because that my memory was slipping? Some memory experts call it as memory overload for people over the age of 60. After all, there is a finite shelf space in brain cells and the storage start filling and crowding from the age five or six. No wonder, by the age of 60, some items start falling off the shelves, if not properly placed. But I take no comfort in it yet.

Over the years, the class attendance is getting worse. Out of 27 students, only two have attended all the classes. Story is different in the larger group. The room is an auditorium with 150 seats. The US students like to sit in the last rows and do not want to be noticed. I use document projector to write on a big screen. There are too many distances between me and the students. It always bothered me, as I grew up in a different time warp in Bathinda.

During my college days of the 1950s in Bhatinda, the relationship with professors were so close that quite a few times, we, the students would go to their homes for help on certain math problems. I was never unwelcomed. In this respect, Hans Raj Gupta, Professor and Head of Mathematics Department (1902 -1988) simply stands out for compassion and concern for his students. He loaned money, freely dispensed homeopathy medicines for the sick students. Above all, he listened to any kind of problems. He was also a father figure to the faculty members in a newly started department of Panjab University, Chandigarh. He knew the names of all his students and would engage each and every one while analyzing a problem. He never solved a problem straight, but extracted a solution by engaging the students. Generally, it meant only one problem in 20 – 30 minutes. But, it opened the windows of my mind forever! I have been using his style of instruction to a large extent. In the US culture, the students, particularly in the 21st century, like to be indifferent, distant, and aloof. Most professors take to teaching like a business.

Such was the mental tape running in my mind, as I noticed three exits for Mesquite. Nevertheless, this whole scenario wanted it to be spelled out in a black and white reflection.

May 12, 2012/Aug, 2014

EASING AWAY FRUSTRATION

(A HANDOUT TO THE STUDENTS OF CALCULUS III)

"Write in 250 words, +/- 5 words your moments of joy, excitement, frustration, and anger associated with this course - implying **aahas/ oohoos**. Also, include words of advice for future Calculus III students with respect to preparation/prerequisites for this course, study habits, homework, attendance, strategies for taking quizzes/tests, course organization etc. Include whatever helpful suggestions come to your mind.

"It will be a good set of pointers for some of you, who may like to re-take this course for a better grade. For your information, nearly 25% of the students repeat it. Your ideas will be put together and shared in the spirit of *The Top Ten of David Letterman*."

During last spring semester, teaching Calculus III started weighing rough on me as well as on the students, though for different reasons. Despite the incentives given to perform better on tests, the class progress was not tangible. The main reasons are students working full time and taking too many courses - excepting two students; only one of them had perfect attendance.

It is becoming increasingly clear that motivating students is essential to classroom instruction. At the undergraduate level, clinical teaching is dry. I hate it personally. At times, I felt like those sport coaches, who fail to inspire their players. It seems as if the game psychology has passed by them. Fortunately, in academics, a different batch of students comes just after a semester. It is hoped that the new batch may respond better.

The following feedback was received three weeks before the semester was over. I tend to think that the generation of students 20-25 years ago was mathematically better, or the change is reflected in terms of social changes in attitude, work ethics, expectations, attendance, and work hours. However, the tests that I gave 20-25 years ago were more challenging. Last Spring, the class GPA was 1.81/4.00; only one student out of 23 students earned an A grade.

Any way, here is asset of collective advice from the students to the students. Some students gave 2-3 pieces of advice. It obliquely reminds me of the TV ads in which lawbreakers advise on good citizenships, burglars on home safety measures, ex-alcoholic to alcoholics, and so on! The old-fashioned advice from the parents and teachers is out of the picture! However, I will take whatever it would help my students in learning the material and pass Calculus III. Here goes the raw pieces of advice; the number before it is the number of students who gave it:

9. Attend all classes.
9. Do homework regularly/every day.
6. Work very hard.
4. Read Chapters before and after class.
2. Work on the material every day until all details go into your blood.
2. Make friends, they are useful/Join a study group.
2. Do not work fulltime and take any other course.
2. Take advantage of extra credit offers.

Do exercises on your own.
Do a problem in different ways.
Find something you like and connect it to the course.
When in doubt, ask question.
Take time to review every day.
Read ratings of Calculus III instructor.
Do not fall behind - Stay current.
Review all test material before exam.
Clear your social and family calendar.

June 11, 2012

A MANTRA OF GOING PREPARED!

'Going prepared' is a commonly heard expression in American life. In any kind of board meetings, the members listen to those who come prepared on the agenda items by checking out on a few facts and asking insightful questions. Furthermore, the companies run around frequent off site meetings with clients, and inside ones with managers and co-workers. Going unprepared could cost in terms of contract losses. Above all, good decisions are made in the committees, when all the members have done their homework before the deliberations begin.

It turns out that this cardinal formula is nearly lost in college teaching. This approach alone sets high school teaching apart from college teaching. These days eighty percent of the college students don't take even 10 minutes to glance over the material to be covered during the very next class. Sadly, 50% walk into the class without fully understanding the material explained in a previous meeting. Such study habits may be acceptable in humanities and social studies, but they never work in mathematical courses. This attitude in a mathematics course, particularly during a summer session, simply does not work. Here are **two** basic expectations from an instructor's perspective:

1. Stay $\epsilon - \delta$ ahead of the class material. It is easy to read in advance a few pages, as if the textbook belongs to ENGL 101/102, where reasonable comprehension is expected. A typical American math textbook has more examples than can be even nibbled. Think over one example before working it out or studying its solution. Highlight the confusing parts or steps. However, make sure that they are cleared up when that material is covered in the class. This should not take more than 10-12 minutes on the average, provided the prerequisite course was passed with at least a C Grade – not too long ago, but only a semester before.

2. The second expectation is that you stay abreast with the class material on a daily basis. A rule of thumb is to **study for two hours on the same day for every hour in the class**. In a nutshell, make sure that the concepts, techniques, and problems discussed in the class are fully understood.

This is just a prep-up e-note before we meet on the first day. Come to the class with a sort of pledge of allegiance/resolution on completing this course. No one is forcing it on you, except your chosen program of studies. Together, we can make it as unforgettable, as was your first date, first drive, or first swim etc.!

Feel free to email me back using Rebelmail only. Good luck!

June 24, 2012/Aug, 2014

COMMENTS

Good points, Satish. If I had my way, the high schools would not be allowed to teach calculus. Too many of my Honors Calculus I classes were spoiled by those kids who took calculus in high school and learned nothing more than the tricks and short cuts. They make the kids who did not take high school calculus believe that these other kids were smarter because they know the tricks. Give me kids who took solid geometry and analytic geometry in high school because they will be ready for calculus. **Paul Aizley**

Dr. B, Your two recent messages have set me to thinking. I agree that motivated students often do well, and that unmotivated students will do poorly. I don't agree with the contention (if I interpret your words correctly) that this is a phenomenon more often seen in college than in high school. I have been teaching for somewhere between 55 and 60 years. Just a few of those years were at the high school level, and about as many were at the elementary level, but most of my experience has been fairly evenly split between junior high and college level teaching. As I have seen it, junior high students are at last as likely (and probably more likely) to "go unprepared" as college students, and I doubt that high schoolers suddenly change their stripes.

My belief is that we're into the second or third generation of a society where knowledge is not valued. One indicator is the frequency of hearing from a student, "I wasn't here for the last (pick a number) class periods. Did I miss anything?" I submit that this is nearly as common at the college level as it is at junior high, except that at the junior high level you sometimes hear it from the parent as well as from the student. When the founders of our country---Washington, Jefferson, Madison, Franklin, etc.---were formulating the constitution, a great many of the general population had two things in common-----they had little or no formal education, but they were skilled at reading, writing, and arithmetic, and they were familiar not only with the Scriptures, but with the writings of such thinkers as John Locke.

We live in a society where attending school is the normal expectation, and there is little or no disgrace in coming out practically unchanged. It seems to be a real shock to 095 and 096 students that they won't be passed just because they pay tuition and keep a seat warm now and then during the semester. Case in point---a 095 student told me during the third week or so of last semester that she really needed to pass the class, adding that it was her third time taking it. She told me that she had had both algebra I and II in high school. When I told her that it was clear from a recent quiz that she really had to get a handle on fractions, her response was, "I don't like fractions." I told her that she didn't need to like them, but she absolutely needed to be able to handle them in any computational situation, and that tutoring was readily available. She scored 29% on the final.

We have many in college who aren't going to benefit from the experience. Some lack the necessary intellect, but I believe at least as many lack the work ethic that it takes to master college material, especially math. Between social promotion and dumbing down the requirements, we have created a student population where mediocrity is often both the expectation and the norm. **Owen Nelson**

YOUR TURN: ONE EXPECTATION!

In a certain phase of life, teaching a math course is like preparing a gourmet meal. The chef of a known restaurant has a name and reputation for a specialty food. If a diner just walks in without any knowledge, appreciation or curiosity of the cuisine, then he/she may be disappointed or turned off from the entire dining experience. It is better to do some homework before making reservations. We all know it, when it comes to fast food eateries!

Last semester, based upon the comments made in student evaluations, given at the end of the course, it made me wonder as to how come some of these students did not check me out before registering in my course or discuss their concerns and expectations with me as soon the course started. With internet technology, we can reach each other before the course starts.

Here is how I decided to approach this scenario: Tell me how your expectations would change between instructors - one who has been teaching for 5-7 years and me who started fulltime college teaching in July 1961? Either, you can thoughtfully respond it or recall it from an actual experience of having two such instructors in high school or college.

I am very proud of my record of college teaching in different countries, different cultures and different education systems. Fifty years does not mean that the first year has been repeated 50 times. Here, no one or two years have been repeated! As a corollary, I have taught 50+ different courses at UNLV alone. To put it in perspective, most professors retire after teaching 10 -15 courses in their lifetime. In addition, I have designed and taught 15 new, experimental courses and Honors seminars. To the best of my knowledge, no other faculty member comes close in the entire university. All this keeps me oxygenated intellectually.

Another corollary of this intellectual diversity is that I have three books recently published and the fourth one is on its way. The first one is **mathematical**; the second, **historical**; the third, **philosophical**; the fourth, **religious**! Before the first class day, check me out through friends, internet and my books. You will experience mathematics as never presented before. It is in a holistic manner – that is life is all about.

I want your comments in about 50-100 words - telling me **only one thing** you would expect from me – yes, only one. The chances are your Number 2 or/and 3 may be covered by someone else's Number 1. Focusing at a point is a great mental exercise. Writing is the best way to train the mind in the art of focusing. You can respond it by Rebelmail or turn a comment sheet in the class. **This exercise is not mandatory**, but you will realize its worth at the end.

July 07, 2012

COMMENTS

Salish, you have a special relationship with your students, which is heartening to see! All the best. **George**

Good idea! That's one thing I miss about your courses--perspectives from your vast array of cultures, experience, people, and situations. Hopefully, your future students will also appreciate that. **Aaron**

TECHNOLOGICAL SURRENDER!

At every turn and stage of life, staying ahead or even staying abreast is always gratifying. For a person with such a mindset, naturally lagging behind in a routine walk eventually begins to gnaw the inside. In academe, a perennial debate is the use of technology in mathematics courses. Ever since the 1970s, when calculators were handily available, I was neither their strong advocate, nor a diehard opponent. This issue gets hotter at the time of exams. Here, my stand was that I could frame the test problems in a manner that the calculators won't be helpful enough, if there was no understanding of the theory behind them. Since I have not taught math courses below calculus for a while, any number crunching aspect of problem solving is minimized.

Personally, I have not used calculators, or softwares – like **Maple, Derive** and **Mathematica**. The main reason is that when I was active in traditional research, my work was theoretical - though, classified as applied mathematics. I never explored its computational and numerical sides. It was conditioned by my mathematics training in India of the 1950s - using paper and pencil only.

Apart from pedagogical side, there is an overwhelming justification for doing arithmetical calculation mentally, as such; the internal calisthenics energize the brain cells too– as claimed by brainteasers and **SUDOKU**. I tell my students that you need not spend money on such games. Just randomly play with a math problem and go as far as you can without writing anything. Being at 70+, I do need to keep my brain cells from getting prematurely fatigued. There are clear signs of 'slugginess', when it comes to recalling the names etc. in split seconds. For instance, until a few years ago, I could keep pace with the **JEOPARDY** contestants – but, not anymore!

Lately, with the advent of smart phones, iPads and other hand-held computing gadgets, I have been feeling helpless in testing the students. Some students have e-textbooks loaded up on their tiny PCs. That rules out any definitions and examples on tests. In math, if you do not understand definitions and statements of theorems 100%, then you can't go too far. Also, math is never understood by reading it or watching someone doing it. This principle applies in any sport too!

Academic cheating has gone so high-tech that some faculty members are literally duped. During a test, students can scan and photograph test problems, send their images to their friends and tutors, and get their solutions in seconds. In order to thwart it in remedial and 100-lever math courses, Math Dept has purchased nearly 300 simple calculators essentially for 'psychological' reasons for the students who want to use them during the tests and placement exams.

I tell my students that the essence of mathematics lies in mathematical thinking - embedded in its deductive reasoning. I don't penalize for minor arithmetical errors. It is time to keep the smart iphones, iPads, Notes and such other gizmos shut off and miles away during tests and quizzes.

July 28, 2012

COMMENTS

As a matter of fact, my Math 128 lectures on the overhead were electronically photographed by one of the students who was positioned in the center of the room. I let him do it because I thought at the time that it would help. Not all of this new technology is negative. You obviously have a negative viewpoint of it. As an old experienced math teacher, I feel it is our duty to see if this stuff can be used productively in the classroom. -but not on testing, of course. **John Green**

Thanks for sending your good valuable notes from time to time. I and my colleagues all relish the humor of your mathematics. **Man Mohan**

No surrender! Well done! An Indian apprenticeship most valuable for many, of our vintage. Regards **George**

Think it this way - the modern generation has very few thinking - the art of thinking for the sake of thinking has been lost - because the computer thinks instead. I mean - compare with the era of Aldous Huxley or Bertrand Russell - they were thinkers. No more - thinkers are no more. Instead, very good and fast computers experts are there. The past gives us some much to read - what would future give us. If lack of technology bothers you - think that nobody can think like you. Keep on trucking. **Subhash Puri**

I agree with you on non-use of calculators and computers in most of the pure math exams. I allow their use while a course is being taught, and there are some problems, which will need repetitive and long calculations - for example, in computing curvature of surfaces, but NOT of curves. But in the exams, I do not allow the use of any electronic machine-help. Regards, **Ravi Kulkarni**

"Math is never understood by reading it or watching someone doing it - like any sport!" Yes! I always say that same thing on the first day of class. They don't let the students use those small calculators in Math 96. I wish they would allow them to. Nice article! --**Zach Porter**

Good analysis. I agree with you on most of the analysis including the case against use of latest technology for testing and assimilation of the knowledge of Mathematics. At the same time, I also believe firmly that time is always with the new generation in most situations. New generation prevails. This includes their moral values! Last 100 years saw too much newer technology and very little newer science in comparison. **Sohan Jain**

PERSONAL REMARKS

FOCUS-HARVEST-SALVAGE

This weekend is very crucial for studying Math 283 (Calculus III) before the last test. At this stage, you may feel that you are in one of the following three situations. The material is fully in grasp; it is slipping out of the grip; or it has completely slipped away. Remember, the time to drop the course is well past; your money is gone. So, get the best out of the situation you do not want to be in. How is that possible at this stage?

Well, I am reminding you of what I cautioned or advised you a week before the course was to begin. Specifically, not studying for two hours for every class hour, holding down to a full time job, or taking two courses in a five-week session, is not a recipe of success in this course. We know mathematical success is subjective. Any way, here are a few study tips for the final week:

1. It is time to stay calm – I really mean it. Do not blow your top as a way of letting off steam. It never works in math. In sports, the players and coaches often motivate themselves by showing temper publicly. It is ruinous in math, as math is different. If you are not in control of yourself, you won't be in control of math problems – it is as simple as this.

2. Do not skim or skip the textbook pages randomly, as you work the material of Chapter 13. Nothing like the material of Chapter 13 is encountered in Calculus I or II.

3. Whatever time you have in one sitting for doing problems, work them out in their entirety. Each problem should open a window of understanding a little wider. Do not try to knock away problems. Do little, but do it very well – it works always.

4. Even when you are not working out the problems, let your mind stay on math concepts and problems. It is a time of assimilating or meditating on them. They will become more digestible and comprehensible. For instance, try it while walking to your car or from parking lot to the classroom or work place. In fact, take walks for 10-15 minutes after working for two hours.

5. Here is one last incentive for you to work smart. If your performance in Test #4 is really outstanding, then I may enhance one of your lowest test scores. That is a part of my teaching philosophy to help my students realize their potential. This is one example of my taking two steps for your taking one step for yourself.

6. Now the ball is in your court, play it with a renewed spirits. Feel free to communicate with me and your classmates you study with. Do not let any problem hang over your mind for too long.

Aug 04, 2012

PS: This ***Reflection*** is partly prompted by a student cussing and shouting F- words after the quiz was given out yesterday. For a 7-minute quiz, he already had 20 minutes, and was the last student holding onto it. I gently said that it was time to turn it in. He angrily got up, slammed the quiz, refused to take a solution sheet, and barged out of the room mumbling. He has a fulltime job and seems in his 30s.

COMMENTS

I don't know what is worse, the cussing and shouting or the crying which is the female approach to the failure on a quiz. We must be strong and wear a bulletproof vest. One of these days, one of the professors at the school is going to get popped off with a gun by an irate student. Unfortunately the sign of the times. Liked this reflection. **Green**

Good tips, funny how many students think they can treat mathematics courses like some other courses (say, business) where you can study the night before the exam and do well! **Aaron**

SECTION II

CONTEMPORARY SCENARIOS

MATHEMATICS OF FUN

Mathematics is fun to do, fun to teach, fun to discover, and fun to apply; that is what I heard in the sessions attended during the annual Joint Mathematics Meetings held in New Orleans (Jan 05-08, 2007). After all, it is *Mathematics Bowl* – like, the *Consumer Electronics Show*, the world's largest convention held in Las Vegas every January.

Since my laptop refused to boot up during the stay, it deprived me of my writing pleasure for three days; the longest gap! Looking back, the prestigious 80th Gibbs lecture was delivered by Peter D. Lax, Emeritus Professor of Courant Institute of Mathematical Sciences. It appeared as if all the 5500 registrants (including 230 from abroad) were in the huge Ballroom to see him, and listen to his talk on, *Mathematics and Physics*, scheduled at **8:30 PM**.

Right after the lecture, a friend of Indian University days and I strolled along the 'famous' Bourbon Street only two blocks from the hotel. Hardly 50' wide and half a mile long, the Street is studded with friendly bars, adults clubs, cozy restaurants, boutiques and various gift shops on both sides. The crowds of people young and old, men and women were seen having fun hysterically as midnight was drawing. However, any comparison with Las Vegas Strip is like watching a high school football game vs. an NFL game!

We settled down in Jamal Jazz bar and music. My friend is a Jazz aficionado, but I let the music jazz my mind while sipping the Irish coffee. Math and music may not appear that close in action, but mathematicians don't miss having xxx-fun when it is in the neighborhood of mathematics, as a needed diversion! The lifetime memories of men are always xxx....! I can't extend it to women. Incidentally, the only book that I bought from the Meetings exhibit was *The Mathematics Behind the Music* by Leon Harkleroad.

A highlight of *Mathematics Bowl* was the joint (AMS, MAA, SIAM) recognition for undergraduate research. This year, it was conferred upon Daniel Kane a Princeton University senior for his ten sterling papers published/accepted and six under preparation/submission! He is neither a recent immigrant to the US, nor the son of an immigrant. He is a true product of the US high school system that is often decried! At least, I am no longer going to be overly concerned about my math students' performance! We also know that mushrooms like Daniel Kane do not grow alone. Future of mathematics in the US is safe

Recognizing new talent and peers for various achievements defines American culture. It is reflected in creativity explosion in every walk of US life. However, it is still not seen in Hindu culture where humility reigns supreme. Humility in an individual is a short-term virtue; collectively, it is a sign of lifelessness! Leadership is nurtured by encouragement, and Indians, by and large, have a very long way to go.

During the joint award ceremony, the **MAA Distinguished Service Award** was bestowed upon 92-year old Lee Lotch to standing ovation when he went up to podium with a walker. Perhaps, he was also the oldest person to present a paper. I felt honored by his presence during my first **Power Point** paper presentation, '*A Diversity Perspective*' at the MAA session on '*Building Diversity in Advanced Mathematics*'.

Naturally, while applauding others, you also dream and envision sitting on the recognition podium one day. A career in classical research was never my professional choice. In 1974, when I joined UNLV, mathematics department awarded master's as its highest degree; the PhD program was started in 2005.

Yes, teaching has been my forte, and this is locally recognized. However, if my passion and prolificacy for *Mathematical Reflections* continues like that of Lotch, then national recognition may come my way! The uniqueness of these *Reflections* lies in personal encounters, historic observations, and cross cultural comparisons and contrasts, all kneaded and braided into every aspect of mathematics. It is motivating me to get the first volume out in 2007! [Note, 06/12/14: it was eventually published in Nov, 2010]

Coming back on the trail of Consumer Electronic Show, there is real and virtual presence of Bill Gates. Mathematics Meetings do not have this star power. The annual prize winners and keynote speakers are like the new electronic gadgets and products of the Show. It would be great to have these two conventions held in Las Vegas. It has been my perennial suggestion to the math organizers.

My charter membership in *Philosophy of Mathematics* is another reason to go to the Meetings. A paper on Euclid Geometry and an invited lecture by A. K. Peters were very incisive. Peters studied logic, did PhD in complex analysis, worked for *Springer Verlag Publishers* for 15 years, and now owns AK Peters, a publishing company especially for mathematics books. His remark, *proof of a theorem exists if it is communicated* and other anecdotal comments were very interesting and stimulating.

The heart of the conference lies in the diversity and quality of research papers (a total of 1800) presented in more than one hundred sessions. Papers were on exotic applications of mathematics spread over several sessions. Karl Schafer's presentation on *Dancing with Mathematics* was attended by over 100 persons with no standing room! He jointly owns a dance company and all dance choreographies were derived from mathematics! He demonstrated some movements with his troupe members. It was aha! My thought was that the day is not far off when fun and laughter will be described by a mathematical model. Then we shall be able to distinguish a genuine smile from a synthetic one!

Jan 12, 2007

COMMENTS

Really Good reflection! Regarding humility in Hindu culture reigning supreme, I ask in all humility: What had you been drinking when you put that thought on paper? The products of Hindu culture that I have met in my life are full of themselves, never tired of being boastful - - while their contempt for their successful compatriots has been contemptible - - leaving out the stars they dare not touch.
Harbans

Very informative and interesting. **RAJA**

Great Bhatnagar Sahib! I am looking forward to publication of your first Volume of Reflections. A few that I have been privileged to read are thought provoking indeed. Always. **Manmohan**

BRINGING THE TWO TOGETHER

Sometimes, it takes too many dots to make a connection between two events or concepts. A month ago, my Department Chairman, while working on my annual evaluation, inquired about a low student evaluation of 2.91 (on a 4-point scale) in a particular course. He knew it was seldom less than 3.0. Chairman being a statistician, I jokingly said, it was a bad data. On a related note, two months ago, my daughter told me that she was going to send her son (my grandson) to a private tutorial center for raising his math skills. The reason for not coming to me was that I was not helpful! These scenarios have been on my mind for a few weeks that they just clicked.

Teaching an academic discipline or coaching an athletic activity involves more than competency on the part of even seasoned instructors and coaches. Assuming, all know their trade well, yet the results are different even in similar societies. In authoritarian cultures, the fear factor may bring the best out of the students and players. In free and affluent cultures, the rewards are taken for granted. It becomes far more challenging to motivate especially in academics. Stakes being higher in athletics, coaches, like Bob Knight, can yell at their players. However, Jimmy Johnson, the winner of two Super Bowls with Dallas Cowboys, could not turn Miami Dolphins around. In a free society (though, its limit is lawlessness), freedom has taken new dimensions - challenging the authority, bending, or breaking the rules with impunity.

Consequently, teaching in the US public high schools is filled with horror stories. During the last 33 years, I have watched teaching taking dive in the colleges too. Las Vegas may top it, as nearly every student works for 30-50 hours a week while carrying fulltime course load. This semester, in an upper division course, three students told me straight that besides an hour or two, there was no time to discuss a problem before or after the class. Last semester, I provided several extra credit opportunities for students to learn beyond the textbook, and make up for their poor performance. But in the semester ending course evaluation, no one even appreciated my extra efforts. The alarming feature is that they are all math and science majors!

My grandson is maintaining a 4.0 GPA in high school. Three months ago, he came up to me with 6-8 challenging math problems, given for extra credits. I tried to 'teach' him how to analyze a problem, 'parse' it into smaller ones, and 'play' with them. Consequently, only half the problems could be done in an hour. Sensing his restlessness, I told him that my doing his problems won't help him in a long run. In trying to raise his conscience, I added that it would be 'unfair', as other kids do not have this advantage.

A few days later, I called him for discussing a homework problem on the phone. In fact, when he was 5-8 year old, we played 'phone' jeopardy by exploring right answers of questions on varied topics. But a 15-year old, in the US, lives in his own world. In India, I learnt in high school out of fear of punishment from the parents and teachers; in college, with sheer hard work - without a word of any encouragement! However, I have taught my US-raised kids and students with incentives and motivation. Perhaps, it is time for me to learn the latest in motivational psychology and new instructional techniques! If not, it is time to hang up the gloves.

March 07, 2007/June 2014

COMMENTS

Dear Uncle, I have not been able to read one of your reflections in a long time. I just noted some comments and have reflected myself. I wish I could present more of my thoughts, but I have to go study. Expressing few of my thoughts during my break has helped me relax. ...

When a student is learning how to write, sometimes it is best to take someone else's words to find your own. I do not have a strong background in math or any discipline that requires problem solving with numbers. However, I have learned in math or any other subject that observing another person's technique of tackling a problem illustrates how you should go about it on your own. As a result, after practicing for long hours, nights, and months, one may find their own method of attacking a problem. I feel that utilizing my own methods of learning and combining it with the techniques of others, allows me to absorb more. The problem today with teenagers, myself, and some graduate student's sometimes is if we have the will to do all this.

In addition, I have learned in education that not all students can meet at the same wavelength as their instructor. At the collegiate level and high school level today, this might be due to a lack of effort. On the other hand, I have noticed those who put in so much effort but cannot for some reason meet half way with the instructor. Sometimes the answer to this might be that it just is not the right time for them. They may require a certain foundation that has not developed yet, or they just simply learn in a different manner. This presents a prolonged discussion in education today, which relates to learning by implementing "fear."

In the medical school I attend, a Pakistani instructor believes that learning is not achieved by creating fear for the student. She feels all too often instructors instill this fear in their students and in the end; it slows down the students' performance. While I agree, you probably do learn more not being stressed, yet if you are too relaxed then this is not an exemplary way of learning either. This discussion might be different in various disciplines, but in medicine I believe there should be fear because physicians must be able to provide short concise answers and be able act quickly. Today, we might need a combination of fear and relaxed learning. **Sundeep Srivastava**

Satish Ji, It is unfortunate for the new students that they can not see the advantage of learning, even when encouragement and incentives are given. Challenge that if we do not perform, we will be out of school and perhaps without a future made us work hard. However, even more so, we thrived on challenges. We wanted to show ourselves as well as others that we can achieve. Unfortunately, this generation thinks they should be handed out everything...and even with that, they are always complaining about working hard. **Prafulla**

So now, what are your new techniques Nana! **Anjali**

My experience exactly. Most if not all students in Las Vegas work from 20 to more than 40 hours a week and their freedom to pursue academic interests suffers. On the other hand, there is much to be said for working and studying as an entree to the working world. I found that a handful of my students were exceptional as "students" despite the workload they carried. But to my knowledge, few of them enjoyed promising academic or 'real world' careers. Now that I live in a more traditional academic town, I can see the difference. Oregon State is heavy in engineering, the sciences and agriculture and the students seem to come from a different planet than those in Las Vegas. As I am fond of saying, we escaped to reality. **Robert Moore**

CALCULUS ENCOUNTER OF A KIND

Sometimes, it takes a while for various pieces to fall in place in order for them to make some sense. About three weeks ago, a person, never heard before, surprised me during a phone conversation, when he asked me, **what calculus was,** as soon as I had told him that, I was a math professor. He described a string of people including his valedictorian son and a math professor appearing on National Public Radio who were all stumped by this question.

I explained to him that calculus is the story of division by zero, which is forbidden in high schools. Then I added that calculus alone explains how average velocity becomes instantaneous, and gives insight of **Infinity**. Geometrically, calculus is the story of tangent at a point on curve. I felt good about this 40-minute mathematics conversation with a layman, and subsequently e-mailed him my classical reflection, *Calculus Defines Civilization*.

After 8-10 days, I ran into this person at a Bone Marrow Registry Camp. There were quite a few persons filling out the forms and getting tested. Soon after getting acquainted, he started telling the same story of people nonplussed by calculus. I was perked up that he would conclude it by crediting me for all the explanations I had given him.

It really surprised me when he didn't say a word! I gently reminded him of our phone conversation over calculus. Here comes the shocker, he publicly denied it! Well, I did not simply want to let it go off and thus gave him 2-minute dressing on calculus again that may have benefited some people who may not be there for calculus!

I kept wondering at this behavior. Yesterday, a retired physics professor, and witness to this encounter, complimented me for my answers and shutting that guy out. Suddenly, a typical Indian mindset bolted my mind. My generation of Indians had a convoluted intellectual training. It was a caricature of what happened in the social circles of British intellectuals during early 20th century. It is outsmarting others by shutting them out.

Now, it is called a conversational brawl. You ask a question and then start laughing, slithering, or turning the eyes around when the question is about to be answered. Yes, for such people, asking a question is considered smarter than finding or understanding its resolution! For instance, this person, over the years, perhaps never cared to figure this question out by going online, visit a library, or even study a popular book like, *Calculus for Dummies*!

As I put this whole picture together, so many scenarios of my Bathinda college days of the 1950s swirled across my mind. Having trained to listen as a toastmaster for eight years in the US, and communication influence of its culture, my Indian or pseudo British show-off side is all buried away. However, the psychologists assert that nothing is forgotten forever; since there exists an incident that can trigger the reversal. Any way, this understanding has cleaned up my slate. Hail thee, my goddess, The Beautiful *Calculus*!

July 15, 2007

COMMENTS

Entertaining story! I've also had that inquiry about calculus--seems so encompassing, difficult to explain to the average person. Hope your summer's going well. **Aaron Harris**

Yaqeen mahkam, amal paiham, Mohabbat fateh-i-alam;

Jehad-e-zindgani men Hain yeh mardon kee shamsheeren.

Translation: In man's crusade of life these weapons has he: Conviction that his cause is just;

Resolution to strive till eternity; Compassion that embraces all humanity. (Iqbal) **Rahul**

This happens often enough. **Ved P. Sharma**

ELEMENTARY CALCULUS IN NEWS!

Last month, the College Dean shared his concern over high percentages of dropouts, withdrawals and low grades (less than C) in the development courses - identified one each from Biology, Chemistry, Math (181) and Physics. It is the first time that it caught the attention of a dean, though an old phenomenon. To my amusement, Geosciences, the fifth department in the College, does not have any developmental course. It is not surprising as Physics, Chemistry and Biology alone are considered as traditional disciplines in natural sciences. Mathematics is their language; mother and nurse too!

Since UNLV is celebrating its 50th anniversary, it is befitting to give some history of **Elementary Calculus I (MATH 181)**. As trivia, its old course number, 121 was changed to 181 in 1990, and the prefix MAT to MATH in 2005. I first taught this course in 1977, though joined UNLV in 1974. Since then, it has been taught 11 times in a lecture format without requiring any math software. The following data is only drawn from my sections, but staggered over 30 years. They do suggest some trends. Besides, it is good resource for the new faculty members to align their expectations with UNLV students.

	Drop %	Full Time %	Sci/Engg %	Math %	Freshmen %
1977 (Fa)	24	30	73	1	uk (unknown)
1984 (Fa)	22	29	50	0	36
1991 (Fa)	30	30	50	4	65
2002 (Sp)	38	uk	uk	uk	uk
2007 (Sum)	20	20	30	0	12.5

The following questions are pertinent to this data:

Is MATH 181 a freshmen course?

MATH 181 is not a freshmen course at UNLV! A sprinkling of freshmen students do take it, but by the time most of them finish it with a grade of C or higher, they are juniors! It is compounded by the centralized advising that the basic science and engineering courses can be taken without calculus first. The Catch-22 is that finishing calculus delays taking the major courses.

Where are the Math majors?

The students (7-8), who commit to math either, they do by an elimination process or suddenly turned on by a math course or an instructor. Rarely, freshmen declare math as their major.

Who are the current stakeholders of Math?

They are no longer historical partners – Physics and Engineering. But, it is the growing number of students from pre-professional areas (namely, Biology, Chemistry), and even business.

Drop Rates

No matter how does one cut off the grade roster, the percentages have not fluctuated much!

Work vs. Courses

UNLV students place equal, if not higher, priority on their jobs over the courses. Over the years, the number of MATH 181 repeaters has increased to nearly 50%!

However, it is better to work with this Las Vegas education culture than trying to change it. After all, UNLV is situated near the heart of world famous, Las Vegas Strip!

Aug 26, 2007/ July, 2014

COMMENTS

Same story (in general) nationally!! **Raja**

Satish, Hope you are fine. Our new semester has just started. Could you please remove me from your mailing list for the daily reflections?

Thanks, **Mohan Shrikhande,** Mathematics Professor, Central Michigan University

I wrote: Hey Mohan *Pyare* (dear), what is this?!

Your name is no longer on my mailing lists of *General Reflections* and *Hinduism Reflections*.

However, before I remove it from the list of *Mathematical Reflections* (average once a week!), I would appreciate your favor of giving me **two** good reasons for it.

I can indulge in asking you for it, as we have acquainted for over 40 years; though not as regular friends, but never on unfriendly terms either. A reason being that I am thinking of having these reflections published very soon. If there is something that professionals like you find it unworthy, then I sure would take it into consideration. I leave for India next Saturday; hope your Las Vegas visit was refreshing. Thanks.

PS: 07/03/2014: I never heard from Mohan again!

TEXTBOOKS AND CULTURES

One of the Contributed Paper Sessions during the 2008-Summer Meeting (called, Mathfest) of the Mathematical Association of America (MAA) is, ***How to Get Students to read the Text and Does this Matter?*** The topic stirred my deepest memories on textbooks as a student and faculty member since mid-1950s, when I was still in India. The noticeable differences are due to cultural and economic factors besides diverse education systems. It is fascinating to reflect on this time line.

The national trend amongst the US undergraduate students for not using their expensive textbooks is partly due their high school instruction formats and minimal study hours in colleges populated with growing number of working students with families. UNLV student body fits into this mold. Last week, in a ***College Algebra*** course, I quizzed on two examples right from the textbook over a day-old material. Result; only 1 out of 70 got them right. Obviously, the rest did not care, or had no time at all.

In India, we used to chew the problems not from one books, but from other problem books. School and college education was a privilege. Textbooks were relatively lean and mean; one or two examples, lots of problems, no modern frill of pictures and diagrams. We sincerely revered our books to the extent that if accidently a textbook was kicked, the Hindu students, in particular, would respectfully pick it up with both hands and touch it with foreheads a couple of times as a sign of penance. Books, storehouse of knowledge and grace of Saraswati, the Goddess of Learning were imprinted in our mindsets.

After all, I have spent 53 years of my college life as student and faculty member in India, Malaysia, and the US. Extreme attitudes of students towards learning from their textbooks have been witnessed. The scenario takes a new dimension when it comes to predominantly working students in commuter campuses like **UNLV**. However, the focus of the paper remains on the US.

This spring, I am teaching two sections (out of 20 offered) of *College Algebra* (MATH 124). It draws students mainly from the colleges of Business, Hotel, Health, and Urban affairs. A parallel course, *Precalculus I* (MATH 126), with identical pre-requisites, is designed mainly for the students in the colleges of Education, Sciences and Engineering. At UNLV, different textbooks are used due to some differences in topics and rigor. Obviously, the dual credits are not allowed.

Last time, I taught *College Algebra*, it was 18 years ago. The noticeable changes in the textbooks are their heftier prices, and heavier to carry them around due to 25 % more pages! The power of computer graphics enables the printing of more beautiful color diagrams and pictures. I don't miss pointing it out to the students that it is all due to mathematics functions that they are going to study.

The homework, being no longer graded and online services now available for homework, it has adversely impacted the use of textbooks. Why the students should study the textbook when the assigned homework problems are not going to be collected, graded and returned in a traditional manner. Here are some incentives used for getting the students consult their textbooks:

1. Use the textbook for discussing particularly the **word problems** in the class.

2. It is my stated policy not to discuss examples in the class. Students are challenged to figure them out! But that is not enough to motivate them. For the last several years, in all lower division courses, it is announced on Day Number One, that every test shall have at least one **example** right from the textbook. Does it push the students to work the examples out? No, in *College Algebra*, it hardly works for 10 % of the students!

3. In the lower division courses, I have been choosing the test problems right out of the textbook. The point is if they have done each and every problem from the textbook, it is good to reward them.

4. The other is an **open book quiz** on the material covered during the last two meetings. It entails some logistic problems, whether the quiz is scheduled, or not. Students end up taking double the time. They waste time in turning the pages for hunting down either the quiz problem or a similar one. Only a little initiative goes in working it out. Yet, it is manageable in a 75-minute class.

5. A couple of days ago, I invited additional ideas from the students that would prod them to study their textbooks regularly. It did not elicit any new ideas. Yes, one un-tried idea is to include **write-up quizzes**. Ask the students to write 200-300 words in the class on a question related with the material covered in a specific chapter.

The more mileage the students get from a textbook, the more likely they are to keep it for future references.

April 13, 2008/July, 2014

UNIVERSITY OF NIZWA, OMAN

(Reflective Remarks at the College of Arts and Sciences Meeting)

Friends, *Assalaama Lekum* (Arabic Greetings)! Also, I convey to you the greetings from my Department Chair C-H Ho, Dean Wanda Taylor, Provost Neal Smatresk, and President David Ashley at UNLV.

Sinbad of Oman is known as the legendary sailor and adventurer in the world. However, he and I do have a common streak. Since 1961, starting full time college teaching, I have moved my households 12 times, taught in four different countries, and have visited 40 countries. Doesn't it qualify me as an academic Sinbad?

Actually, my claim does not stop here. At UNLV, I have an unofficial record of having taught 50 different catalog courses both at the graduate and postgraduate levels. Besides, I hold another record of having designed and taught 15 experimental courses and Honors seminars. They are popular with curious students and engaging faculty. The administration always supports innovation in instruction.

Teaching different courses to different groups has been my forte. Six weeks ago, when Prof Ahmed e-mailed my teaching assignment of three different upper division courses, I did not present my wish list before or after, as always done in the US. As a kind of corollary, let me frankly say, that though my teaching load is 50% more than at UNLV, yet I accepted to teach at University of Nizwa (UN) for tasting new academic and social culture. To top it, it is being done at a salary that is 50% less than at UNLV!

However, my life is all about rich experiences and memories, and that is what I wrote to Dean Ismail in a *Reflective* note, last October. No matter what our roles in life are; at home, as a parent, spouse, or sibling; outside as neighbor, colleague, or politician, no one wants to be forgotten, when the inning of life is over. Nevertheless, one is remembered proportionate to his/her legacy.

Mathematics is now a paradigm for me, a window to the extent, that it drives my life! Please count on me as a guest lecturer in classes, speaker at students' campus events, or substitute instructor, in emergency. It is a common practice at UNLV. For instance, I left the US on Nov 15, three weeks before semester ended. One graduate course (means post-graduate at UN), I covered through e-mails, and for the undergraduate one, I paid a substitute instructor out of my pocket for six lectures. Of course, the Chairman and Dean were duly informed.

My current interest in mathematics is no longer partial differential equations for which I earned PhD 35 years ago. Mathematics is a bit like football (called soccer in the US). If 35 years later, someone asks an aged member of 2009 Omani Football Championship team, "What you do for living?" Do you think he would ever blurt out that 35 years ago, he was on an Omani championship team? Strictly speaking, hardcore research in mathematics is like heavyweight boxing; one is fundamentally done by the 30s.

History of ideas and history of mathematics engage my mind these days. A month ago, I gave an invited talk at the national conference (Dec 19-21) of the Society for History of Mathematics, held in Imphal, India. To the best of my knowledge, Oman is not on any academic map of the world. Let us try putting at least UN on it by forming, say, professional associations, chapters, getting international accreditation, developing twining programs with other universities like UNLV, and holding conferences on the campus, etc.

Please feel free to exchange ideas over Omani coffee for which I want to develop the taste before leaving in five months. **I**, indeed, try to live life as an intellectual Sinbad!

Jan 20, 2009 (Oman)/Jan, 2010

TECHNOLOGY: A STATE OF MIND

The US, in particular, exports 'formula research and knowledge'. For example, countries like Qatar and United Arab Emirates that hardly had high schools 50 years ago, have building complexes, like cyber cities. One of the corollaries is that the West can easily sell systems of communication, life styles, and health care in the name of technology transplant. It is a myth that one day these countries will also make scientific inventions.

These thoughts burst out today after 6 weeks of nagging frustration with three technology babes; internet for staying connected with my world outside Oman, internal e-communication, and students' e-records at the University of Nizwa (UN). Prefacing the technology transfer problem, it took two weeks for my desktop to be installed in the office. In the meanwhile, my colleagues let me check my e-mails on his PC. In this part of the world, nothing gets done by yelling at people. Literally speaking, I haven't seen people any where shouting or being angry at each other. There is an Islamic culture behind it.

A festering problem is when suddenly the G-mail does not stay connected even for a second for two days in a row. The weird thing is that 'google.com' does not open up, but 'google.com.om' does. There is no problem with the Yahoo on campus. Off campus, there is no problem with the Google either. Everyone on the campus has been aware of the Google problem for months, and they only bemoan about it. Either they have decided to live with it, or have no expertise to fix it up. The American mind sets itself apart, when it comes to solving problems.

Coming back to my Gmail saga, the click sequence - Google Preference, Gmail, Page—Invalid, Google Account, G-mail settings, loads my emails to disconnect it right away. It reminds me of a hilarious commercial featuring a former US presidential candidate, Bob Dole on men's Dysfunctional Erectile problems! The crash prompts a message to sign in again! After 4-5 trials, I shut the machine and walk out of the office. It often works the next day!

The Dept Head, a 67-year old retired professor from an Egyptian university (Moscow PhD), moved to Oman two years ago. He really disarms me with his smiles and coolness. A 25-year old secretary has been on her first job for four weeks. Dean's secretary, in a US system a little 'god', did her bit for me in another IT problem. Of course, the Dean, a 60+ Sudanese, an algebraist (UK), is aware of the problem too. Incidentally, the Dean and Head separately observed my teaching in different classes on a student's complaint. They promptly acted on an Omani student's concern, but the issues of foreign gypsy faculty remain unresolved for weeks! Well, I asked for it; at least, get the best *Reflections* out!

The college coordinator, an Omani young man, hardly 30 year old, is 'powerful' at the UN. His office is better furnished than that of the Provost at UNLV. Thrice, I met him, and he called IT experts and an assistant dean. Once, after seeing the 'crash' problem in my office, he contacted an IT 'guru'; but no resolution. Apart from e-mails, I can't access the list of my students for keeping their records on tests, quizzes and attendances etc. But this reflection is a byproduct of this aggravation.

Mar 02, 2009 (Oman)/July, 2014

COMMENTS

I always like your notes. Hope you are having a great time! Even as we turn our gaze inward, our future lies in looking out as you have noted. Best wishes

Neal Smatresk, Former Provost and President at UNLV, and now President of North Texas University since 2014.

PERSONAL REMARKS

MY ENCOUNTERS WITH EGYPTIANS

There is a buzzword around the University of Nizwa (UN) that faculty hired from Egypt dominates the campus. It reminds me of the state of Haryana before its creation in 1966. Its level of literacy was very low, as the local people, mostly called the *jats*, like the Omanis, are born warriors. When Kurukshetra University became full-fledged university in 1963, most of the faculty came from the neighboring state of Punjab. The states of Haryana and Himachal Pradesh were taken out of the larger Punjab state.

In the Arab Muslim world, the Egyptians carry the image of experts in Quranic as well as modern scholarship. At the UN, I have known three of them. However, our acquaintance has not gone beyond knowing each other's names. They are polite and cultured, but a glass wall seems to stop them from socializing – like even having a cup of tea together.

This afternoon, on finishing a *Reflection*, I was in a mood for tea. I rang up the door of Khaled, who lives in the adjoining flat. He is PhD, about 40, and teaches education technology. For long, we have been going in the same university bus three times a week. It was a weekend afternoon, but he kept thanking and saying, "I am tired, at some other time etc.". His dentist wife and two kids are staying back in Cairo.

Ahmed, 67, PhD from Russia, lives with his wife on one floor above mine. He joined the UN in 2007, and was appointed as the Dept Head last year. Once, we reminisced non-alignment years of Nasser, Tito and Nehru. A couple of times, I invited him too, but politely he withdraws. I don't mind it in a new culture. With age, one collects everything - including data, and the human brain loves to fit them into a pattern for a possible explanation.

Said is the third Egyptian, in his 50's, and we share an office. He did MS from the US, but returned to Egypt for PhD. The course work and written compressive exam before thesis discourage many people to do PhD from the US. I have met several Indians working in Oman without PhDs. They talk of going to India for PhD registration, and essentially finish it in absentia. The PhD requirement for jobs has dropped its standards significantly in India particularly.

Said's wife has a math PhD too, but lives in Egypt with four kids. Since we are together, small and medium talks are unavoidable. Whenever, I offer him snacks I like to munch in a break, he politely declines. Every 20 minutes, he would utter 'Hi Allah', and any time he goes out of the office and comes back, he would softly whisper, "Dr Satish!" They are his subconscious vocal stretches. Our apartments are within 500 yards of each other, but we have yet to meet outside our office.

Am I imposing any kind of social obligation or expectations on them? By any Indian or US social norms, it is no. The Americans would drink and have small talks even with strangers. Here, the Omanis live in their own exclusive world, and the non-Omanis have no world! It is this type of unique cultural experiences that I have been having besides the educational ones.

In 1968, I 'befriended' with an Egyptian graduate student, in his 30s, doing PhD in linguistics while working as a parking lot attendant in Indiana University campus. His brief hi-bye association just flashed my mind while trying to recall all the Egyptians I have personally known in life so far! This human sample may be small, yet statistically significant.

April 09, 2009/Oman

MANAL: MY OMANI ROYALTY

Recognizing distinguished students, staff, faculty, administrators, and alumni is a sign of an established university. Every US university/ college proudly lists its over-achievers. The University of Nizwa (UN) is very young - only 4-years old private university (not the same type as a private university in the US). It has already carved a niche in Oman when it comes to recruiting students, particularly girls from Omani royalty and nobility. I am sure the faculty and administrators are hired to match the high expectations that their parents may have.

Within 2 weeks of my arrival on the campus, I heard from the Dean and two department heads about a girl, from a royal family, attending the UN. It is a part of the culture to watch the interests of such students. It reminds me of a twin daughter of President Bush II who broke the family tradition by not attending the Yale University (private), but University of Texas (Public). It is said that besides her security staff, hardly anyone knew her on the campus, as she never flaunted her presidential lineage.

One day, while talking with the Math Dept. Head about the said royalty girl, I said, "She is in my classes and her name is Manal." He said, "No, her name is such and such…(I don't know)". Just at that very moment, Manal walked into the Math Office. Very gently and cautiously, I asked," Do you have any direct or indirect connection with the Sultan of Oman?" She said, "No, but I know that girl," She responded. Nevertheless, I told Manal that she would remain my Omani Royalty!

The folklore attributes associated with girls from royal families are--- beautiful looks, fair complexion, and unmistakable grace in gait, conversation and manners. Subjectivity apart, Manal has plenty of these traits. Every 10-12 years, the Mathematical Association of America launches a campaign against the myths that girls are not good at math, and beautiful girls never study math. My data of the last 48 years, spread over four countries, statistically rejects the first hypothesis. On the second one, math generally thrives on introvertedness, and beautiful girls nourished on attention and extrovertedness, make the pair of math and female beauty, a psychological rarity. However, Manal is, indeed, a counter-example.

This semester, she has finished four upper division math courses and one, *General Physics* with lab. It is an overload by the US standards. However, three courses taken from me alone are for 'mature' math students. Normally, the courses on *Linear Algebra II*, *Number Theory* and *Group Theory* are taken after finishing *Calculus III*. Manal was ill advised to take them concurrently with *Calculus III*.

In each of my courses, her grade is above the class average. In *Group Theory*, she scored the highest in the Final Exam that was semi-comprehensive. **My mission at UN was to turn at least two students out of 25 into thinking persons**. With Manal being Number 2, the mission is accomplished! I have told her that she is bigger than any college diploma.

Her 'Royal' touch: Once a quiz/test is finished, she never sits over it, but gracefully floats out of the room. Manal is destined to make an impact on Omani life. She is one of the girls that a man never forgets. Thank you, Manal, and the UN for the lasting memories!

May 27, 2009 (Oman) July, 2014

COMMENTS

The Reflection -- capturing the subtle yet significant change in lives of people -- was worth the wait for Omani reflections. **Harbans**

I thought the 'myths' of female underachievement in math have been mostly debunked: http://www.nytimes.com/2008/07/25/education/25math.html

Still, stereotypes prevail in most cultures, including the US. That is why math & engineering oriented companies like Google have a '*Take Your Daughters to Work Day*'…in an effort to reverse the trends. The connection between introvertedness and math achievement (in females) is an interesting one. **Avnish**

Yes, there was on Manal whom I taught. I think it may be the same. She has already graduated. They all come and go and some leave a footprint and others are forgotten. There are some students who wish to keep in touch with their teachers even when they have left the Uni. for good. I have admiration for such few ones. **Abraham**

ADVISING: A FOSTER CHILD

To be in absolute minority of one or two is an experience by itself. It tells that either one is living in a dark age or in a futurist dreamland. In a participatory US democracy, one is called upon to vote all the time. Technically, democracy could be a rule of a 51% majority over a 49% minority through a term that can change at the next balloting. However, in the history of mathematics, one person alone has been right on more than one occasion. **Mathematics is not democratic – it is logic!**

Today, undergraduate advising was an issue at the faculty meeting. A moot point was whether math majors are to be advised by math faculty or by the College Advising Center (AC). My suggestion was to have a split advising. The AC advising was OK during the freshmen and sophomore years, when mostly general core courses are taken up. Once the students are math majors, they are juniors and have taken at least two calculus courses, it is then that the math faculty should be assigned to each major. At UNLV, there are hardly thirty math majors that equal to the number of math faculty. Whereas, seldom more than ten finish the math bachelor's in a year. Mostly, the students switch to math after getting turned off by science or engineering program. Undergraduates form a nursery of any graduate program.

It appears that the present faculty do not want to deal with undergraduate math majors! At the beginning of fall semester, the Department circulated a list of all graduate students and graduate faculty advisors assigned to each of them. The number of students doing MS or PhD is nearly 50 : 50. Like in any math graduate program in the US, at least 80% of the graduate students are from foreign countries or from out of state. The 'home-grown' students are in a small minority. Las Vegas culture does have an impact on the choice of majors. That is why early nurturing of math majors is pertinent.

However, universities, like UNLV, are transitioning from predominantly teaching to research institutions for a number of reasons. Its Math PhD program is only four years old, but expectations in research and grantsmanship have been rising incrementally. The administration is lax about the undergraduates, though lower division math courses provide all bread, butter and milk to the entire university. One of the reasons is that the state resources for undergraduate education are also allocated to two other state supported colleges in the Las Vegas area.

UNLV did not have any doctoral program when I joined it in 1974. The faculty followed the progress of their math majors. There was no AC in the entire university; now there are a dozen of them – in every college! Centralized advising is one of fattest layers in higher education. Advising reminds me of a common scenario in the US life. The dentists, primary physicians, pediatrics, ophthalmologists, podiatrists, they all want their patients to visit office every 3-4 months, whether they have any problems or not. Whereas, most Asians go to a doctor only if there is a medical reason. Now the physicians curtly refuse to see such 'irregular' patients. What a contrast with the world of academia!

In times to come, a professor may retire without having ever advised a single undergraduate! In the context of mathematics, a PhD faculty member may not be competent enough to direct a math thesis even if a research paper has not been published during the last 2-3 years. Nevertheless, if the heart is in the right place, through advising, he/she can touch and transform one life at a time.

Nov 20, 2009/July, 2014

COMMENTS

Very interesting and enlightening... **Aaron**

Satish: Good points. We have 93 undergraduate students majored in math. We advise all of them. I asked secretary to assign students to faculty members for advising. I leave the tenure-track faculty members alone. You can image how many one has to advise per year. I never hear any complain about this. **CS**

Have you shared this with the math Faculty? **Neal Smatresk** (UNLV Acting President. Since 2014, President of North Texas University)

That's the conundrum I'm currently pondering as I will go back to Malaysia to begin my career as a mathematics educator (teaching future math teachers in Malaysia). Yet, I myself have never gone through any teacher training programs since I have been teaching math to college/univ level students. In addition, there has been a discussion at the faculty level that the degree in teaching is no longer the focus, but will consider more of the postgraduates who have been teachers and wanted to come back to upgrade their qualifications. Yet many lecturers, like myself, have little experience in training (or supervising) experienced school teachers. ha ha.. **Rohani**

I went to a small private college---St. Olaf College in Northfield, MN, 2700 students---and my memory is that nearly every prof took an interest in me and offered advice. I don't remember a single PTI or adjunct prof other than one who was a retired school administrator, and his class was the least useful of any class I had in four years. When I decided to major in biology, the head of the department became my formal advisor.

During my eighteen semesters as a PTI in the math department, I have had dozens of occasions where students indicate that they feel as though they are assigned to classes in a willy-nilly fashion. Some have been enrolled in 122/123 when a teaching career is the farthest thing from their mind. I currently have a student in 096 who is also enrolled in an advanced class in Boolean logic, for which he is woefully unprepared. It was well into the semester before he told me about it. When I asked why he took such a course, he said the only reason was that it was what he was told to do so by an advisor. **Owen Nelson**

CULTURE AFFECTS CREATIVITY

Yesterday, during midnight hour, I called Professor Ram Parkash Bambah in India. The recording at his mobile phone said that it was not equipped to take the incoming calls. At one of the two landline phone numbers, the person who responded was his domestic assistant. Bambah, perhaps, extended his stay in Hyderabad after attending the International Congress of Mathematicians, held there two weeks ago. He taught a paper (two-semester course) in *Number Theory* during the second year of my MA (1960-61), exactly 50 years ago, from Panjab University (PU), Chandigarh.

It was a different era and culture. The relationships between teachers and students were not fleeting. Once, Bambah took me from his office to home while discussing some problems. The downside to this relationship is that it is always one way - whether in respect or communication. My call was triggered on his turning 85 this month. Being in my 70s, while the news of an old timer dying jolts the sense of mortality, but a person, like Bambah, active at 85, inspires nonetheless.

I sat down to recall all the instructors who taught me math during my undergraduate and graduate years -both in India and at Indiana University (IU). From the undergrad years (1955-59), in Government Rajindra College, Bhatinda, of the two instructors, VP Bansal is deceased, but SC Deva, now a widower, remains energetic at 78. His conscientious teaching, in a lax Indian academe, has rubbed off on me. Deva avoids his PC, and rarely picks up the phone.

From the PU years, HR Gupta, SD Chopra, IS Luther, RN Kesarwani are all Gone. About DD Joshi, I have no idea. He wrote a letter of recommendation for my admission to IU. TP Srinivasan, at 78, is in a frail health. From my IU days, Halmos, Hopf and Leonard are no more - no knowledge on Hornix and Wonnenburger, Brothers and Lowengrub. However, JB Conway is on my mailing list.

The most vibrant communication that I have is with RP Gilbert, my PhD supervisor. He left IU in 1974 for a chair professorship at the University of Delaware. It was also due to a testy divorce. Friendly divorces are myths; or they exist in the movies. My quote on marriage and divorce is that, "Marry a girl for whom you may kill someone, and divorce a wife, if you feel like killing her." Gilbert always encouraged me to continue collaboration in his research areas, but after PhD, I felt like a cork going off a champagne bottle. I became intellectually wild, and UNLV environment has been conducive.

Thirty years ago, a physics colleague opposed the faculty hiring of an Indian applicant. His reasons shocked me then, but make sense now. He told me that a junior Indian colleague kept a distance due to overly respect for age, status and seniority. **These factors are inimical to free exchange of creative ideas**. He added that fundamental problems are generally broken down in relaxed atmospheres, like over beer, chicken wings and boobs (turned into Hooters Restaurants, 25 years ago!).

Over the years, I have tested this hypothesis many times. In India, it has led to incestuous researches, dead ends, and weak math organizations.

OK - fifteen more years to go, Bambah, as he is commonly known in India!

Sep 04, 2010/July, 2014

COMMENTS

Dear Satish, Usually, I do not promptly reflect on your reflection but this one was irresistible. It was because of R. P. Bambah was in Hyderabad. It was nearly 55 years ago that I attended my very first conference in Hyderabad, and that of Indian Mathematical Society. Then President of Indian Mathematical Society (IMS) was Ram Behari, who was my Ph. D. advisor and an iconic figure at that time. His tenure as the President of IMS lasted longer than usual. I made my first ever presentation. I followed a senior and experienced colleague (also a Ph. D. student of Ram Behari) who fumbled under a question by TIFR (Tata Institute of Fundamental Research) Ph.D. student, much to the consternation of our esteemed professor. Fortunately, I stood my ground and being the youngest participant, I came out smelling like a rose.

Coming to the main point, it was then I met Bambah in Hyderabad. He was impressive in more ways than one. He was young, handsome, intelligent, and imposing figure. Late Hans Raj Gupta made a popular presentation and so did Late P. L. Bhatnagar. Late R. Krishnan (a prominent Physicist and a protégé of Late Sir C. V. Raman) gave a talk on non-Euclidean Geometry!! In all, it was one of the most exciting experiences for me.

I am copying this email to Mangho Ahuja, who attended ICM 2002 at Beijing with me. I will give details of ICM 2010 in Hyderabad later. I can mail one of you a spare copy of each of the daily newsletters, which were published in my presence. (I left a day earlier.) Let me know who would like to receive first and mail it to the other. I will try to do it at the earliest, but I will end up mailing right after the election. Will you be attending AMS meeting in New Orleans? With best, **Subhash C. Saxena**

CONVERGING LIVES

While driving me to Palo Alto, my son casually inquired about TP Srinivasan, whom I was keen on meeting during this trip to California. Last year, the meeting did not plan out. What can you tell to a US grown person in a few minutes about a person with whom the main association is that he had taught me complex analysis paper (a two-semester sequence) during my master's in 1960-61. Since leaving India in 1968, we have met only once and, perhaps, exchanged a couple of calls/letters.

Generally, communication between an Indian teacher and Indian student is like a one-way street. Nevertheless, the powerful Indian culture steeped in ancient *guru-shishya* (teacher-taught) tradition nourishes this bond subterraneously. In today's Facebook culture, such an association is inconsequential. I don't think that any one of my students, taught since 1961, would ever take efforts to visit or call on me just for the sake of it.

However, I told my son that TP also 'taught' me how to stay relaxed during stressful exams by going on long walks. Also, two vivid memories that stand out are of an evening, when he invited his students over a dinner. It was April, 1961. TP was not married then, but had a house servant. As I entered his university accommodation, I was awed by a full size Hindu temple enshrined in one large room. For reasons deeply embedded in the history of India, the north Indian Hindus, in particular, started having tiny temples in the closets, shelves, windows, or cut-outs in the walls. A bit funny thing was that a temple has to be in a Hindu home, and yet out of sight of the visitors. But TP's personal temple was really magnificent. As a devout Hindu, he daily prayed before the deity and applied a small ritual mark on his forehead. His pride in his religious practices was unseen amongst the so-called intellectual Hindus of the north.

TP's originality spelled out in the kitchen front too. As we were enjoying a sweet dish, he challenged all the students to identify any one ingredient in it. Obviously, sugar, water, milk etc. were all wrong! Later on, he explained the recipe - they were all almonds with peals beaten up and stone grounded for seven hours turning the raw almonds into a paste for cookie cuts. The almond oil breaks out and brings in the moisture. The almonds were so expensive then, that eating one a day was a sign of family status! It was the last time that I ever had that dish. In the US, one can find white almond paste without peals, but it has traces of preservatives.

An hour that I spent with TP and his wife was like visiting a temple. You show your respect and move on. At a ripe age, some individuals are no less than the idols and temples. Indians routinely go for the blessings and simply sit in their presence. There is an entire **DARSHAN** philosophy behind it. For the last five years, TP has been inflicted with Parkinson's disease affecting his movements and speech. Having been a man of few words, now he speaks with great difficulty. I told him about my first book published. His wife took out TP's 1988 textbook, **Measure and Integral**, co-authored with JL Kelly. Some men take more pride in their books than in their kids. The books stay longer while the kids move out in their worlds! Generally, it often takes much longer to bring out a book!

His wife told that TP has remained between 115-118 Lbs. all his life, ran several marathons, ate small and right; yet, diabetes caught him 20 years ago. Life is strange. Amazingly, TP never had a PhD, but had guided several PhD students in University of Kansas and Panjab University (PU) Chandigarh. In mathematics community, he is known for publishing alternative and elegant proofs of theorems already published. TP has known India's Prime Minister Manmohan Singh since he joined the Economics Department of PU in the 1950s. They remain good friends.

Interestingly enough, TP and Manmohan Singh both visited my friend and me over lunch in September, 1964. My friend was a student of Manmohan Singh. We both taught in PU Evening College Shimla. Life is an album of memories. Thanks TP! What a coincidence that as I turn 71 this week, TP turns 78 next week.

Dec 14, 2010/July, 2014

PS: 07/2014. TP gave up the ghost last year.

HUMANIZING MATHEMATICS

The *Humanistic Mathematics* is one of the oldest contributed paper sessions of the Mathematical Association of America. Its two sessions were organized during the Joint Mathematics Meetings, held in New Orleans–during Jan 06-09, 2011. The diversity of papers was very wide indeed.

The thrust of my paper, *Three Humanistic Approaches*, was to '*humanize*' mathematics for students, who particularly struggle in a dozen of remedial and lower division math courses. For instance, they can't comfortably relate with, say, a technique of completing a square, quadratic formula, bunch of trig formulas, rule of integration by parts, or with definitions like that of a group or vector space. 'Relating' means to be able to share and talk about classroom mathematics with family members, friends and fellow workers. As a matter of fact, it is a challenge even for math professionals when it comes to presenting everyday importance of mathematics before the lawmakers and civic groups.

However, this goal of 'humanization' is significantly achieved by 'shifting' the focus from specific math courses to the life at large. Then, solving math problems becomes microcosm of facing problems never handled before. That is the story of any individual life. Furthermore, the qualities–like patience, practice and perseverance, needed in working math problems, are demanded in a theater of life too.

Over the last two decades, a basic template of humanizing mathematics for most undergraduate courses has crystallized. That is the heart of the paper presented. It mainly consists of writing three 250-word **extra credit reports** -worth up to 3 %. The Report #1 is Self-Analysis of Test #1, given at the end of the third/fourth week, but never later. The student must introspect and rewind the mental tape to carefully examine their performance - why it was excellent, failing, or anything in between. It is due within 72 hours after the Test #1 is returned. In sports, the coaches analyze the games next day after the games. In life, one learns from only those mistakes that are not forgotten. Nearly

80% of the students write it, and at least 90% of them get higher scores in Test #2. It is at this point that the remaining 20% of the students indirectly realize the importance of Report #1.

The neurologists tell that the human brain is activated 70% of the times with visual images. The present digital technology has pushed it a step further - that human beings can learn any subject by watching the right videos. The Report #2 is written after watching a video. It is never a summary, but a critique of only one of the excellent mathematical videos – like ***Mathematical Mystery Tour, A Beautiful Mind, The Proof of Fermat's Last Theorem.*** They are now available on **YouTube**. These videos shed light on the nature of mathematics, and mathematicians working on varied problems. The students are literally wowed and awed by this experience. Generally, they discover a new 'perception' of math and mathematicians, which may rub into a math course at hand. Report #2 is collected after the 8th/9th week of the semester.

Report #3 is a granddaddy of all. It is briefly explained on Day Number 1, and its importance is gently stressed throughout the semester. Its whole objective is to connect the knowledge gained in a specific math course with **any activity the student is passionate about** – be it, another course, skill, game, hobby, or job. This report is due within 72 hours after the Final Comprehensive Exam is taken up. At this stage of studentship, any connection is great - if none, it is no less important too. It is the mental effort that counts. Basically, the students are sowing the seeds of interdisciplinary thinking in their minds. Life is all about networking – be it between human beings, ideas or any resources.

Nearly 80 % of the students do Reports # 1 and 2, but only 30% submit Report #3. It may be added that these reports are like points on a line of life continuum. At every opportunity, life values are interjected in mathematical scenarios. For instance, in tackling problems, where, say, a right choice of origin, axes, or coordinates, helps in simplification or finding a solution, it is immediately connected with right choices or right values in life.

Like in any aspect of teaching, not every student captures the humanization moments in the class. At the end, in course evaluation, there are a couple of students who consider my sidebar remarks as wastage of time. Personally, four decades of active living with mathematics means that mathematics has become a paradigm of my life. I enjoy understanding life through the power deductive reasoning, and thus share it passionately with my students.

Apart from these reports and 'sermonizing' remarks, a 5-7 minute quiz is given on non-mathematical material in textbooks–like biographical and historical notes. The textbooks are getting heavier and students' attention span shrinking, who then has the time to read even small well thought-out notes on the lives and works of mathematicians? However, I, for one, do take a time to read them loud.

The reports build and refine the writing skills of the students. Nearly 25 years ago, there was a push towards developing special writing courses, or integrate writing in course curricula. Also, these reports are excellent tools and measures for course assessment, which is a buzzword in academe these days.

Well, it is time to put something together that started off undirectionally years ago.

Jan 10, 2011

COMMENTS

Thanks for the ideas in this reflection. I've made some attempts at humanizing (I am more apt to call it personalizing) the math that is being studied, but the approach that you describe is more structured---and very likely to get a trial in my classes this semester. A simple thing I've done several times is to offer extra credit for a written description of at least one way that students have used algebra in the past year. In most classes, less than half turn anything in. **Owen Nelson**

Good idea, Satish, Some students angrily learn "humane mathematics". Their advisors often think it means sticking students by teaching only easy and useless examples. We use the "humane" to mean that it is to help the student become **civilized**. I approve your teaching, **Looy**

Satish Dear- Beautiful - very original. I wish you were teaching when I was doing MA. Actually, even myself - I wish I could be doing Math MA now at this maturity and understanding when I can comprehend almost anything that is written. **Subhash Puri**

A MATH-MAGICIAN I KNOW

"No," said I, when a receptionist at **Regal Assisted Living** asked me, "Are you a magician?" It was understandable, as she explained that most visitors, coming to see Looy, were magicians. Looy, the Lewis Simonoff, was passionate about magic. For 25 years, he taught magic classes in UNLV's Division of Continuing Education, and grew into a scholar magician. It was not a coincidence that at one time, Math Dept had three magicians on its faculty! After all, Las Vegas is the magic capital of world.

It was ten days ago when I Last visited Looy. Otherwise, we periodically spoke on the phone, as he was on my mailing list of **Reflections**. Within a few months of institutionalized living, his memory had a rapid decline. He attributed it to heavy medications administered to him. He was mentally prepared to Check Out from Planet Earth. Looy was 82, when he gave up the ghost during early hours today.

There was something interesting and intriguing about Looy. For instance, he never visited the Dept. or was even seen on the Campus after he retired in 2000. He had joined the Dept. in 1966, when it had only 5-7 faculty members - mostly non-PhDs. At UC Berkeley, he worked on an open problem in an area of mathematical logic for his PhD dissertation. In a competitive intellectual environment in major US universities, as soon as Looy learnt that someone had a solved that problem he was working on, he quit on the dissertation forever. But logic had permeated Looy's persona. He always spent 2-3 weeks on the elements of mathematical logic - no matter what course he taught - from College Algebra to Calculus.

Looy often said that magic is unseen logic. Alternatively, take logic out of mathematics, it becomes magic! He explained mathematical principles behind the card tricks. As a corollary to his love for mathematical logic, he was stickler in English usage – playful with grammatical variations and syntax. He told me of his growing up as a sickly child - thus often was forced to stay home during school days. Late night listening to radio helped him in the development of

162

language skills and other intellectual pursuits. He rarely went to bed before 2 AM.

Looy had family ties with me, as he attended several marriages and anniversaries. Family members remember him for being entertained by his magic tricks. He is one the few men who equally loved to eat and cook. For many years, Looy cooked Thanksgiving turkey at our house. Naturally, he remained a heavy-set guy all his life. Looy's collection of books is so enormous that in order to save moving expenses, he had them placed in a storage. During the visit, when I inquired about the fate of these books, he just waived his hand in resignation. **No one winds up every business before the Time comes.**

However, all the books, videos and magazines that filled two bookshelves in his one-room living space pertained to magic only. Today, I told my students that one must cultivate a hobby or two in parallel to one's (intended) profession. It is important to stimulate and nurture it at a young age. That struck a cord in my mind, as I discover reflective writing enriching my life - never imagined before. Thanks Looy for the memories!

Apr, 13, 2011

COMMENTS

Greetings, Satish.....Hal Whipple forwarded to me your very thoughtful essay about Looy. I, too, have many memories of him. If Bill Phillips were still alive, he would be greatly saddened. If you would please inform me of any plans for a memorial or such, I would very much appreciate it. Best Wishes, **Sue**

This was quite a moving tribute to Mr. Simonoff; so good of you to visit him often. Your words brought back fond childhood days when our family shared special meals with him. Avnish and I were amazed when he once demonstrated a levitation magic act! It appears he went in peace, in his advanced age. Unlike the tragic news received this week. A speech therapist from our dept. was found passed away at her school (cause unknown)- at the age of 33, she leaves behind her 12 year old daughter...When I return from D.C., let's plan a visit with Milly & Leela, it's long over-due from my side! **Gori**

Thanks Satish. Quite touching. **RAJA**

Sorry to hear, you have lost a very good friend. I remember, you talked about him more than a week ago. It seems, he passed away far faster than you thought. The way, he was getting treatment and worsened physical conditions, he is now in a better place. I remember his magic shows. May God bless his departed soul. **Pramod**

Satish: Thank you very much for the kind words you said about my Uncle Looy. We all lost a very good person. **Michael Simonoff**/SG Partners Inc. - The business behind your business.

I'm only in my 11th or 12th year at UNLV, so I have only heard stories about this fellow. Thanks for adding to those stories. With regard to hobbies, I've told many a junior- high kid-----and many a junior high parent---that one of the most important things they might do in life is to learn more about some topic (almost any topic) than any of their peers know. Everyone needs to be an expert in some area. **Nelson**

Yes, another very inspiring story from my friend. Thanks, Satish. Very enjoyable and very well written. Moving emotionally. Did he have a wife and family? **Dutchie**

Dear Satish, I am sorry to learn that Lewis Simonoff passed away. I still have happy memories of his smiling face and the intriguing things about him that I remember after 31 years, such as, his denim over-all with various colorful pens including an ingenious orange peeler, which he deftly handled to peel an orange, some of his card tricks during our meetings etc. I remember the math department secretary (I forgot her name, a middle-aged woman) calling Looy around lunchtime to wake him up so he could come to his class later that day. When asked, "How are you?", he will always reply "Terrible, terrible". May his soul rest in peace. **Rangaswamy**

Thanks Satish – beautifully written – no one could have said it better. **Allan**

Magic effects created by Lòóy have been performed on national television specials by Doug Henning, in stage and close up shows by Lance Burton, Mac King, Paul Harris, Paul Draper, Alan Ackerman, Dan & Dave Buck and more. His most popular magic inventions include Earth Shoes (rock from shoe), Flippant (A card color change), Hamman ESP (mentalism), and Sooperman (levitation). His work in magic can be seen in Apocalypse, Antinomy, the True Astonishment DVD set, Channel One, Best of Friends, Magic for Dummies, Art of Astonishment, Magic Magazine and regularly in books by Harry Lorayne, Alan Ackerman and Paul Harris.

Why did he love magic? "I like the insights into the mind that come from learning to deceive it." **Why perform it for others?** Magic allows us to: "Share a pleasantly magical ambiance of temporary liberation from the tyranny of natural laws. If that isn't enough, it's also a hoot!"

Who is a magician? "A magician is a story teller, he tells you a fairy tale and for a little while you almost believe it." **What is magic?** "Magic is practicing miracles of a semi religious nature with everyday objects. The way people see it and talk about it later on; they magnify it in their minds to a religious level." **Who is your favorite audience to perform for?** "A skeptic who is open-minded"

Do math and magic have anything in common? "Both math and magic are about proving things. Proving to people that something is true." **What is the best way to invent a new effect?** "The way I develop most tricks is that I find something I don't like about an existing trick and I work a way around it. Or turning it upside down, given the magic effect that I want to produce I can often find a way to solve the problem and create the given outcome"

What sparked your interest in magic? "Watching my father present a few tricks and then reading books by Blackstone and Thurston. Later I became a lifelong fan of Erdnase. I would take the train into New York and visit Tannen's magic shop. But as I became more interested in magic my mother told me to stop, as I was becoming a delinquent. (Because I had a relative that was a pretty bad guy who had performed magic as a boy.) So when I didn't stop, off I went to military school and so never stopped."

Where did the name Lòóy come from? "Looy dot dope" (stories overheard through a dumb waiter) by Milt Gross" he continued, "I've even published academic articles under that name." **Who is the best magician that you ever saw?** "Harry Blackstone, the father. He had great charisma and all of those pretty girls lined up."

.Lòóy Simonoff's "**Celebration of Life**" Memorial was held in the Alumni Center at the University of Nevada, Las Vegas on Saturday, April 23

Alan Ackerman performed his version of *Lòóy's Hamman ESP* which first appeared in Ackerman's book "Here's My Card" and Scott Hitchcock performed effects created and inspired by Lòóy with a walking cane. Mac King told the story of first reading Lòóy's Earth Shoes and how it gave Lòóy a god like status in his mind. Mac went on to explain how he and Lance Burton searched for the perfect rock along the water edge in their hometown and worked on the effect together. Peter Reveen, who used to headline in review shows on the strip but if best known as a Hypnotist and Lance Burton's manager shared personal stories about going out to eat with Lòóy after his shows on the strip, as Lòóy always knew where the best-hidden restaurants and finest food could be found in Las Vegas.

The following excepts come from a letter that was sent by Paul Harris and read before the mourners: I would often show Looy some complex routine I was working on...where I was very proud of all its "ingenious" twists and turns. Looy smiled and said "Nice idea..but needs work". I didn't want to change a thing. But Looy gently taught that less is more.. to narrow the focus down to whatever the one most perfect beautiful thing might be, hammering home the rules of elegant construction, the beauty of simplicity, the joys of a perfect fit between form and function. And a bunch of math theory that always left me clueless but would somehow inspire me to reach for the unreachable thing. And I was always astonished at how much better these routines became after an all nighter with Looy. And when more often than not my projects collapsed into a worthless pile of torn bent cards. Looy would always be there to help pick up the pieces and somehow make it seem like it was all a glorious success..and that somehow I'd just earned a golden ticket to some bigger exciting adventure which was just around the corner."

Paul Harris

PERSONAL REMARKS

GLIMPSING SELF-ACTUALIZATION

My classroom instruction is guided by a few simple principles: **Number One** – *a student should never feel that he/she is out of earning a particular passing grade*. During my college days in India of the 1950s, there was no semester and letter-grading system. The raw scores were reported at the end of two years - in a four-year bachelor degree program. When I came to Indiana University, Bloomington for my PhD, one instructor told me, "No matter how well you do in the final exam, you are not going to get an A." It really bothered me, as I was penalized for not having done well during early part of the semester. **This approach is totally unacademic.**

Number Two – Psychology tells that human beings learn at different rates and at different points in time, particularly, in schools and colleges. Personally, I hardly learnt more than 50% during class lectures. My roving eyes being wonderstruck, my mind follows them off the lectures. More specifically, in a class of 40 students, a concept like linearly independent vectors does not sink equally in all brain cells. Two days ago, a quiz problem (MATH 330/**Linear Algebra**) involved an application of the definition of linearly independent vectors. Not even single student got it right - despite a hint! It is the last week of semester, and this concept was introduced in the third week.

I told my students, "If you get a grade of B or higher in the Final Comprehensive Exam, then it may be your course grade - irrespective of your lower past performance." It really fired them up. Of course, it is not announced in the first week. It is done in the last week, when all the tests and quizzes are done. Most students work really hard, pay to the private tutors, and study in groups. It instills a life lesson - *never quit in life*. Americans sports truly thrive on it. There is a popular saying - *It ain't over, till it is over.* My approach is the practice of this *Mantra,* when I tell my students that show me understanding of the material before the semester is over, and you would be rewarded.

This *Reflection* is prompted by today's e-mail from a student who is doing A-level work. His peeve is most uncommon: that why the students, flunking the course, should get a shot at earning an A grade?

For years, I have faced this question. Again, it boils down to my teaching philosophy: *an instructor must help the students to reach their potential*. Once a student has experienced it in a course, he/she is changed forever. And that is greatest reward in the teaching profession. Personally, in 50 years of college teaching, I can count at least 50-70 students (will appear in a book) who have been transformed by my teaching. Teaching touches all the peripherals of life in subtle manners.

I never grade on curve, as it either inflates or stifles the grades at the upper end. Statistically speaking, in a class of 35, only 2-3 students get higher grades based on their performance in my Final. But for a week, it keeps them charged up, and that is the best learning environment of lifetime. Also, comprehensive preparation for the Final goes a long way into their readiness for next math courses.

May 04, 2011

COMMENTS

Always enjoy your teaching reflections as they help those in the practice without as much experience! **Aaron Harris**

SECTION III

ASSORTMENT OF REFLECTIONS

MATHEMATIZATION OF RELIGION

[**May, 2014**: A draft of this paper was written up in 1991. It remained on a back burner for a while, and then eventually forgotten for more than two decades – out of my nature too. It was discovered a few weeks ago while sorting out mathematical reflections, which were saved in many unrecognizable Word files. Going over it, I realized that it merits inclusion - though despite its being unfinished and unclear in a few places. I may go back to it later on.

Another reason for its inclusion is that, who knows that someone may clear it up and extend it further. Historically and to a large extent, mathematics has been enriched by short and long-term unsolved problems. The main point is that mere introduction of mathematics slices into the hearts of complex problems in many walks of life. It works like a hot knife cutting through a slab of butter. Finally, the text that follows is adapted from this draft after a lot of pruning and editing.]

ABSTRACT

The paper attempts to elucidate the complexity of any rituals and beliefs based religions through the language of mathematics. Conflicts and peace are its immediate corollaries. It may be added that a popular term, *Dharm* in Hindu lexicon has rightly no equivalent in English vernacular. *Dharm* capsulates universally transcendent, ethical and moral principles of life in its totality. It is amorphous as compared with organized religions based on their founders and their teachings.

For any mathematical considerations, first in line is the religion of an individual as applied in his/her pursuit of life. Next is a religion of two individuals **not necessarily** between two human beings. It can be incremented to a religion of three individuals, and so on -------. Thus, religion embodying a non-empty set of values/beliefs of an individual is unique. For example, if there are five individuals in a group, then there are 31 *Dharmas* (sets of principles), and their interactions would lead to 930 different (set of sets)!

No wonders, reference to wars, annihilation of the enemy are so commonly interspersed in the Vedic *Mantras*. It has nothing to do with violence for the sake of violence. Then come in natural order the cries for peace and respite from such conflicts. The Vedic *mantras* of *shanti*/peace are not against every violence, war and conflict, but they only make a call for a respite from it.

BACKGROUD

If there is a fulcrum at which Hindu culture and civilization rest, then it is *Dharm*. In the Mahabharata, the great Rishi Ved Vyas defines *Dharm* as the sustaining principles of an individual, society, institution and nation. That *mantra* is transliterated as follows:

Dharanna dharm mittyahu: Dharmo dharayate praja:Ya: syadharan sanyukt: sadharm iti nishchaya:

However, the colloquial use of this word has been equated with the English word religion that is generally identified with major and minor organized religions of the world. The author attempts to show that it is only one of the interpretations of *Dharm*. A mathematical approach makes the understanding of *Dharm* somewhat easier.

Introduction of mathematics in any subject brings ultimate clarity of thought and gets rid of any ambiguity in it. That is the *Dharm* of mathematics! Let us start from an individual, a basic unit of universe. No matter what Hindu definition of *Dharm* one may take from a scripture or scholar, the *Dharm* of an individual is nothing more than a set of his/her sustaining principles. Survivalism is not necessarily supreme or a guiding principle. *Dharm* is unique to each individual, and in fact, its manifestation alone makes one individual distinct from the other.

Let us denote D_{1i} as the *Dharm* of the ith individual in the universe of human beings. The letter D is taken from the word *Dharm*, first subscript 1 signifies *Dharm* of one individual and i for the ith individual. i can be any integer, from 1, -1, 2, -2, ----. Negative integers can be thought of individuals who were alive at one time and positive for the living ones. One need not wonder about the exclusion, i = 0. It could be handled but let us not get into notational exercise.

Let me interject at this point that in the classic discussion of **Dharm** in the Gita, where various shades of **Dharm** are espoused. Vinoba Bhave (1895- 1982) has eloquently elaborated D_{1i} in his classic book, the **Talks on Gita**. He calls it **svadharm,** and further elaborates the follow up actions/**karma** into **vikarm** and **akarm**. The paper is not intended to delve into what goes into the making of an individual's **Dharm.** Vinoba goes to the extreme in laying out that one's individual **Dharm**, called **svadharm,** is waiting upon when an individual is born. However, it also undergoes a continuous transformation, as a person grows. Yet, **Svadharm** is not shifty and opportunistic.

On a personal note, presently my **svadharm** is to leave my environment - including my place of work, living and various ties and bonds, better than I found them. It is simple to state it, yet highly complex when it comes to grapple each noun and qualifier. Naturally, it is likely to come into clash with another person's domain of wellness.

n-**DHARM** MODEL

Before continuing with the mathematical formulation, let us be clear that each D_{1i} is a set of either crystal clear or amorphous beliefs of an individual i. Likewise, we define D_{2i}, D_{3i}, ...for groups of 2 and 3 individuals, and so on. Let us pause to understand these **Dharmas**. In general, D_{ni} stands for the *Dharm* of the ith group of n persons. Creating these notations is not difficult, but their understanding is deeper. However, this mathematical notation does demystify the complexity that pervades **Dharm** that Vyas has indicated. Of course, we are cognizant of the exclusion of an individual's **Dharm** toward his school, colleges, and nation at large. Incorporating all of them is no problem mathematically. Though the intent of this paper is limited, but its scope is very wide.

Let us again fully understand what D_{ni} stands for. If an entire universe is divided into all possible groups of all different sizes then all groups of any size, say having n individuals can be labeled Number 1, 2, 3, ---, i, --- 1000, ---1,000,000, and so on,---, 10^{10}; assuming for simplicity 10 billion is a population of the world. That is a very large number, but for mathematicians it is no big deal! Now for each i, D_{ni} is the **Dharm** of the ith group of size n, which as stated before is a set of say transcendental principles of life. From an organizational point of view, it may be safe to impose the condition that the number of principles gets smaller as n increases.

Mathematics is the discovery of new objects, and the study of their properties after defining operations amongst the objects. What we have is a set called D of various **Dharmas** from a population. Interaction between two groups is guided by their corresponding **Dharmas.** Under a uniform distribution of belief systems, there are equal chances of an interaction could be called a conflict or cooperation.

A **Degree of Conflict** may be defined, if $D_{in} \cap D_{jn} \neq \emptyset$ (empty set)

Peace between D_{in} and D_{jn} is defined, if one is a subset of the other.

SOME OPERATIONS

I tried to define the following operations in D:

1. $D_{mi} + D_{nj} = ??$

2. $D_{mi} - D_{nj} = ??$

However, it is plausible to visualize that $\bigcap_{n=1}^{\infty} D_{ni} = \emptyset$ and $\bigcup_{n=1}^{\infty} D_{ni} = D$.

This mathematical modeling of **Dharmas** seems like an n-body problem in mathematical physics, posed first by Einstein to understand the dynamics of the entire universe. Relatively, Einstein's problem may be simpler problem as compared with n-Dharm problem. Reason being that between two physical bodies, one only takes into consideration the gravitational forces between them. But in the case of two **Dharmas**, there are unmeasurable different forces of various beliefs in each one of them!

The purpose of this paper is not simply to over-stretch the mathematical ideas. The point has been made. Complexity is spelled out. Conflict is inherent and internal in human groups, so is equally the desire to resolve conflicts and bring peace or respite from it.

9/1991 and 05/2014

PERSONAL REMARKS

MATHEMATICS AND RELIGION

Before putting one's thoughts together on a subject like this, and that too in a limited space-time capsule, one has to establish certain boundary parameters. There is a general agreement on the nature of mathematics, and what it stands for at different levels of one's proficiency. It essentially means the same thing amongst people with similar backgrounds. Its practice and pursuit are not different in different lands and cultures. Religions, however, reflect the social, political, and economic conditions of the land of their birth, adoption and practice.

Mathematics has progressively established a universal identity. However, religions tell different stories. They are very different; big and small in terms of their followers; old and young; founders and without founders; tied with one scripture, or free from them; birthdate or none; and so on. History of organized religions essentially portrays that the outer form of religion is a conglomerate of disjoint modules sparingly connected. Yet, they profess some unity, perhaps, in the spirit of human race. In contrast, edifice of mathematics is like an inverted pyramid; solid, shiny from every facet, vibrant, and has been reaching out to newer heights literally at a ceaseless pace.

God is the central concept in all religions. They all conceive, perceive and are centered around God – though, in their own manners. Therefore, it is essential to have some functional and rational agreement on the notion of God. After all, if something has been a part of human heritage for ages, at least, I tend to believe, that there has to be some cumulative force behind it. It simply cannot be rejected. **Personally, for me, belief in religion, consequently in God, is to bind my physical, mental or spiritual endeavors with higher cosmic source of energy.**

One's progress and evolution in religion or godhood can be discerned in terms of 'harmony' around that person. It is often described by an aura of the person - a kind magnetic field. I do not mean to interpret harmony as the absence of conflict; but, certainly without obvious contradictions. In science and mathematics, order is the absence of disorder or chaos during a particular interval of time and space. It is easy to measure one's research achievements in mathematics - say, by the number of research publications (one of the modes of making it public).

On the other hand, it has been said that the 'enlightened' individuals, in supreme spiritual states, become deaf, dumb, and blind. It means that the direct experience of Divinity or Supreme cannot be described by any sensory modes. Furthermore, any attempt to explain it leads to ambiguity and eventual contradictions. **In the super sensitive state of mind, the Observer interferes with the very process of Observing the Object!** It is akin to the **Heisenberg Principle of Indeterminacy**, or the consequences of **Quantum Probability**. However, there is no corresponding problem with a mathematical solution. Any complex solution can be subdivided into comprehensible units.

Rituals and mythologies of religions are symbolic in the sense that they do keep the restless minds and believers on a track. There is a remarkable similarity between ritual symbols in religion and say, algebraic symbols in mathematics. A person who is not familiar with a particular branch of mathematics may not find any meaning in its mathematical symbols and notations used there. For example, very few mathematicians have any idea of the work in mathematical logic, which Russell and Whitehead put together in their magnum opus, the ***Principia of Mathematics***. Mythological symbols in religion are meaningful to its scholars and believers. If rituals are blindly followed, then they are as ineffective, as they are useless to the non-believers of that religion. Symbols in both religion and mathematics are to be manipulated by certain rules, but never indiscriminately.

Mathematics does not have a God like central entity about which it revolves and evolves. Through its applied nature, mathematics aims on unraveling the laws of the universe. **It hinges on the hypothesis that the ultimate secrets of nature can be understood in a mathematical language.** If the objective of a religion is to communicate with the ultimate truth or reality, then its mathematical form may be one of the modes of this actualization.

That brings mathematics and religion vying to converge at a common goal. The essence of mathematics lies in the power of its deductive reasoning. The question, whether there are other modes of understanding the laws of the universe, remains moot. There is strong evidence that the knowledge of some physical facts has been arrived at without the sophistication of modern science and mathematics. For example, certain Yogic techniques are claimed and acclaimed for training the mind to acquire holistic knowledge of the universe, rather than looking at its one piece at a time, in a modern scientific approach.

The progress in science and mathematics moves in a 'linear' progression that one can measure a distance between the two points traversed. In religion, the movement seems to be in a spiral trajectory. A few centuries ago, say from the time of Euclid, modern mathematics was very rudimentary, but today it has grown into a gigantic enterprise by any standards. Anyone can see its profound impact on other disciplines. On the contrary, from the history of religions, one may observe that the 'understanding' of God has remained constant through millennia. There is a common misconception that science and technology have taken man away from religion and God. In a scientific pursuit, when years are spent in a lab, or in study den in order to find a solution of a knotty problem, then a scientist or mathematician is deeply committed to truth, and that is being religious – nothing else.

The concept of infinity has taken a central place in mathematics ever since Calculus was invented. Mathematicians are very comfortable with the notion of infinity. They are not bothered whether there are infinitely many objects out there. Persons, who are not mathematically inclined, are always uncomfortable with infinity. It is perhaps no different when some people believe in God and others who do not believe in God.

It is not out of place to point out at the paradoxes, like that of Zeno from the BC era. Their proofs on the existence or of not existence are based upon certain conflicting premises about infinity. In Set Theory, a branch of mathematics, one deals with a hierarchy of infinites. **I believe in God as a mathematical limit, or the ultimate potential of an individual's achievements!** The believers in God argue that it is the Grace of God that enables a person to achieve the 'impossible' state. Whereas, a mathematician working hard on it, argues that it is a logical outcome of a long quest.

A question boils down to whether a state of mind exists in which mind transcends itself, and can make certain events materialize at will. **It is a reverse application of mass energy equation of the General Theory of Relativity**. To the best of my knowledge, it has not been lab tested yet, in creating matter out of arbitrary form of energy. The approach of religious believers is of a total illumination of life. Whereas, science begins its exploration, as one sets out in darkness with a tiny flashlight in one hand. One sees only a small area where the light is falling. Other areas remain in complete dark until the light falls upon there. The search for knowledge, with tools of logic and deduction, is a slow process. But it eventually grows like a snowball, provided the process does not stop.

Any small work done in science and mathematics extends the work of the giants in their fields. Differently put, what Newton did in science and mathematics in his lifetime, can be understood by a good high school student today. In the realm of religion, such a claim is very difficult to make. **There is no transfer of knowledge in a hierarchical manner from one 'high' soul to the other**. Religions have inner cores, as far as the knowledge of the Supreme is concerned, but their adherents make it look different by factoring in rites and ritual besides, social, political and economic values. Otherwise, when it comes to the discovery of a silk road to godhead that is a pathless path, as J. Krishnamurti has aptly put it.

In the final analysis or synthesis, mathematics and religion are not poles apart, as their outward forms appear to suggest. Mathematics is becoming religious. A discovery of a mathematical result can be a religious experience for that mathematician. However, any religious experience becoming a mathematical experience is still a remote possibility. It may be an ultimate dream coming true for the Pythagorean School of Philosophers! Mathematics is coming closer to religion in terms of its pervasive presence everywhere, and that is the omnipresence of God according to every religion.

Over the years, these ideas have grown out of literature like that of the following books:

1) Tao of Physics: Fritjof Capra (1975)
2) Gödel, Escher and Bach: An eternal golden braid: Doug Hofstadter (1979)
3) Infinity and the Mind: Rudy Rucker (1982)
4) Chaos: James Gleick (1987)
5) Complexity: M. Mitchell Waldrop (1992)
6) Lectures (in many book forms) by J. Krishnamurti

PS:

This handout was prompted by a student in LBS 711 (a graduate course in interdisciplinary Liberal Studies Program) who majored in religion for her BA degree. It is customized some material to meet her background. However, it was also distributed to other graduate students.

Feb 06, 1995/May, 2014

COMMENTS

1. Dear Satish, Yes, this is one of your very best REFLECTIONS. Maybe the intent was to convince readers about religion and god. In only that respect it didn't work on this lame brain. Thanks for all the information and getting to know more about your personal philosophies. Hugs, Your neighbor, **Dutchie**

I wrote: It means that I failed to convey--- mathematics can give the same high as a religious experience can!

Dutchie: Well, mathematics has been a deep mystery to me. It is a profound lack in my education and in my adult experiences. You are the first Mathematics Person in my life.

2. My dear Bhatnagar Sahib, Namaskar - After a few slightly confusing reflections, this one is simply class. It seems you've started speaking (and thinking) like Maharishi. Though, it may take me a few readings more to fully understand this one. At

the first instance, it is remarkable. Specially all that is written in **bold** font seems to reflect what YOU think. Deep regards. **Jagjeet**

3. Satish, You KNEW I had to respond to this one didn't you ... Practically Religion and Math differ in a VERY CLEAR way. The difference is like the difference between warrior and weapon. The weapon, much like mathematics answers the how of the battle. While the Warrior, like religion, must answer the WHY, and not just the why but also the "why now" and the "how much"

In battle, the weapon (math) has no concern over what we commonly call ethics or morals. The weapon determines how we fight but doesn't answer whether we should fight at all, or if we fight how much of our body, mind and strength goes into it. That is the realm of religion.

Mathematics, however, is not as pure and calculate-able as you would have us believe. The deeper into math you go, the more uncertainty you run into. In fact, you make up oxymoronic mathematical terms like "imaginary numbers" and "uncertainty principle" and "dark matter"

True religion doesn't bind or restrict your thoughts and research into CREATION, true religion encourages digging, searching, quantifying, and exploring because the more you know about the CREATION the more you will get to know the CREATOR.

God's definition is not the sum or potential of human achievement because God cannot be put into a box to be measured, nor can the infinite have borders. All along that inverted pyramid of mathematical discovery you will find God smiling and encouraging because science and math leads people away from God but GOOD science and GOOD mathematics will bring them back again. Keep searching because I believe you are good at what you do. **Steve**

5. Wonderful reading. Enjoyed reading it. I think this is your best reflection **ever**. What a flight of thought! What a clarity. Wow! Afreen Afreen. **Rahul**
6. Dear Bhai Bhatnagar: I have read with great interest all of your emails writings reflecting your emotions and experiences ranging

from intimate groups of your family to your involvement with Hinduism, temple organizations, arranging lectures from scholars and practioners of Hinduism and practicing yoga and now your scholarly masterpiece writing on similarities between Mathematics and Religion. I was wondering what caused this change from worldly wise, politically nationalistic, and devout friend to a soul searching and non-involving in family and friendship bonds type personality. I see a new dimension of your personality which is full of insightful observations and a sharing of your ideas with others.

I look forward to meet with you and discuss our old bonds and the new directions as reflected in your writings. I am impressed. Love. **Kundan Bhatia**

7. Hi Satish: I have enjoyed reading this eye-opener 'reflection.' The 'infinity' you have postulated has that undefinable 'infinity' of Hinduism which explains the 'infinity' of gods and goddesses in the Hindu pantheon--the Hindu minds are open and not constricted by excessive number of prayers and finite scriptures and treatises. I believe the 'meditative' feature of Hinduism allows us to 'think' and 'think.' Fools act first and then think; the wise, on the other hand, 'think' first and then 'act. The 'passivity' of Hinduism has, I believe, has direct correlation to meditation and thinking. **Moorty**

PERSONAL REMARKS

ULTIMATE MATHEMATIZATION

(Letter written to Bhaisab, a saintly figure of Ambala Cantt, India)

Yesterday, I received a brochure announcing your upcoming one-week **Bhaagvatam** discourses. While zestfully going through it, I paused at a point where it read, *that this would be the second time in twelve years that you were giving a public Bhaagvata Sandesh* (message). I re-mailed it to my relatives in Ambala Cantt suggesting them to attend these sessions - particularly, the very first one.

My thoughts flew past the hoary labyrinths of spirituality in India. The Buddhist folklores tell how after 10-12 years of austerities and subsequent enlightenment, the erstwhile crown prince Siddharth came back to public life as Gautam Buddha, and shared his newly found resolution or solutions of human miseries. Incidentally, another contemporary crown prince, Mahavir, founder of Jainism, went a few steps further in this perennial quest.

This phenomenon of public dissemination of accumulated wisdom of any kind is observable amongst the saints, doctors, professors, artists, and even the rich. Explanation is simple: when a pot is full to the brim with any talent, then its contents automatically begin to flow out of the pot, unless there is a leakage at the bottom. The funny thing is that human problems remain the same in every respect, but the solutions come and go with time! An irony is that in India human miseries have touched all heights both in reality and perception. It is no wonder that in India alone, one finds people 'selling' happiness, giving recipes, amulets, and *mantras* to get it.

My thesis is that years of solitude, meditation and contemplation on deeper questions of life, *do endow the body and mind with new powers and capacities*. After all, why it wouldn't? We know what happens to the human body, when one spends hours after hours in body sculpting. Even the tiniest muscle of the body stands out to make a statement. The students, toiling on books, are the ones who end up on the merit lists at the end of the exams. If one works on intellectual activities, one is bound to reap intellectual fruits. It is not suggested that the activities - primarily called physical and intellectual, are very distinct. In my mind, they aren't! It is a matter of putting different emphasis. Perseverance, discipline and monitoring of progress are essential common ingredients.

Now, I come to 'spiritual' activities along the lines described above. Here, one is not doing much of any physical activity. For instance, visualize the 19th century saint, Ramakrishna Paramhans, who was known for sitting in front of his deity for hours. A saint does not pour over books or engage in traditional scholarly activities. In fact, books and bookish knowledge are left far behind. All one may observe from outside is that the master (*swami*) is engaged in some inner quest and dialogue even while surrounded by his/her followers and worldly objects.

There is no dichotomy between worldly or unworldly! It is all one-worldly - called *Advaitya,* the **Principle of Oneness,** in a school of Hindu philosophy. The temporal differences are due to one's introspection and perception. It varies with evolution of a person, and of course, it varies from person to person, depending upon the level of self-realization. Eventually, such a person is going to be gifted with some mental prowess too. The spiritual states - like *siddhis,* are real. You go after a particular mental strength, you are bound to achieve it after years of mental concentration. It is no different from developing muscles, studying music, or mathematics, etc. - a degree of proficiency is reached accordingly.

Let me recall a well-known spiritual incident from your life. I was not surprised when you brought back to life the Radha Krishna devotee, Prema. She was lying hopeless in the jaws of death in Chandigarh PGI hospital. You specifically went there, fully charged with the 'healing power'. Prema, having faith in you, was the right receptacle for the energy that you passed onto her. It is only due to ignorance of this 'spiritual science' that people call it a miracle.

It is scientific, and going a step further, it is mathematical too. The essence of science lies in its demonstrability. It is repeating an experiment under identical conditions and observing the same inference. In mathematics, however, any number of verifications is not a proof. It is the deductive reasoning, governed by rules of logic that establish the truth or falsity of a mathematical statement. I believe that everything has a mathematical form too! It is obvious in science and engineering, but, so far, it seems remote in the domains of theology, or more appropriately, in spirituality.

Let me add a few remarks from my experience and understanding of modern science. *We are all energy/shakti* in the literal sense. What may appear as different forms of matter are manifestations of energy in various states, and are taken up by its dynamic nature. Matter dissolves away into energy over a period of time - from nano-seconds to geologic eons. Einstein proved a famous formula, $E = MC^2$, connecting M (for mass), C (speed of light), and E (energy). The appearance and disappearance of matter is *maaya/leela* – the 'playful' interchange of two states - called *dvaitya,* the **Principle of Duality**, in another school of Hindu philosophy.

Observing from such a grand stand, how can one actually duplicate an experiment in space and time coordinates? The observer, the object to be observed, and the process of observation - including the instruments of observations, all **three** have changed since the 'previous' experiment. Am I then leading to a conclusion that the principle of demonstrability of science is not based on solid foundations? For 'gross' experiments, it has been OK, but not for very subtle experiments occurring in say, *hath yoga*. That may be a reason for the decline of 'yogic science', which dived due to foreign subjugations of the Hindus in their homeland, India, for centuries – until 1947.

On sensory experiences, one willingly pays enormous ticket price, say for watching a nuclear explosion, seeing the curvature of the earth from a thousand miles up in the sky, walking up on the moon, or flying straight above the mouth of an erupting volcano. Also, man wants to go deep into the depths of the ocean to see marine life, and hear the sound frequencies never created, or heard before - so on and so forth. *Is there any law of conservation of our sensory experiences?* Do we gain something at the cost of something else? Are there some Meta sensory experiences?

My personal thesis is that any realizable state has to have a mathematical form too! Since Euclid, mathematics has come a long way. It has already penetrated deep into biological and social sciences - even the fine arts are not spared. *Well, my question to you is how do you analyze your capabilities in a step-by-step manner*? You may try to 'cop' out by saying that you don't have any new powers. However, I have given some reasons for your having developed it systematcally.

Modern science was developed in the West, the yogic/spiritual science is rooted in ancient India. Of course, it did not remain in an exclusive domain of the Hindus - like the study and applications of modern science are not limited to the Christians. At present, without any systematic training, one finds scattered bits and pieces of this 'lost' spiritual science. Like many other pieces of our ancient heritage, this is nearly lost. During the British rule of India, yogic science became synonymous with black magic (*kaala jaadu*). The ancient scripture, *Vigyan Bhairava Shaastra* that throws light on yogic science was pushed underground. On the other hand, the youngsters are trained in modern sciences through universities and colleges.

Persons like you owe a debt to ancient Indian heritage for shedding personal insights on it. What you are going to say on *Bhaagvat* is not going to be anything like what you said twelve years ago. Why the two will be different? The years of silence are going to bring out new originality of interpretation - unthought, unheard and unspoken before! And it shall not be based on your intellectual study of the *Bhaagvat*. *What is this new element that is going to give a new shine?* Certainly, if Buddha, Mahavir, or you, knew any formulas of mathematics, principles of science, or expertise in humanities, then they would be forgotten or regressed for practical purposes. Is that the price for enlightenment? Some transformation does take place within, as the domain turns outwardly macro. Internally - mathematical or rational thinking transforms into non-rational or quantum thinking. Tunnel view changes into universal one. In some terminology, it is called the awakening of the *kundalini*, which bears different names in other cultures.

I do not lay claims in spiritual arena, since no algorithm has convinced me for realizing its powers. However, I have experienced its fleeting glimpses in moments of reflection and concentration. For example, one does not have to understand electromagnet theory to appreciate its functioning in televisions, telephones and sound amplifiers etc. There are three major strands interwoven in this write-up - namely - spirituality, non-rational thinking and mathematical thinking.

Rational thinking appears logical and closer to common sense. It is binary in nature, right or wrong, but silent on the discriminating power that decides what is this, or not-this. It is like playing a little god. In my investigations that is the cause of some paradoxes. However, it opens the door for what may be deemed as non-rational thinking. Its existence is seen in the wisdom of the sages, whose understanding is totally holistic.

While teaching an honors seminar on *Mathematical Thinking in Liberal Arts*, music, visual arts, law and history are investigated on a premise that there is an underlying mathematical thinking. I don't claim that we are able to ascertain it, but the efforts demanded did frustrate students, at times. The manifestations in music, art, law and history are the result of interplay of symbols in a deep subconscious mind. My modus operandi is that *man is one, no matter what is pursued individually in the so-called domain of physical, mental, or spiritual*. There is a common pool of symbols, which are tapped into specific disciplines. If one can consciously access this common pool of pulsating symbols, the *Manasrover*, then one can map out works from one discipline into the other. Isn't this a measure of enlightenment?

Please find time to touch upon the strands of ideas that have come within your spiritual orbits. I'll be eagerly waiting for your **light on the subject** – more than cursory comments. Finally, welcome back to the world after years of seclusion!

March 05, 1999/May, 2014

COMMENTS

H Sri Hari H Jan. 12, 2011

Dear Brother Sateeshji: Jai Shree Hari. I've gone through your Reflections 000, and 577 with interest. I hope the time and brain consuming reflections serve you the purpose you've in mind. All the best As Ever, I'm, **'Bhaisab'**

[**PS**: Bhaisab took his last breath on April 21, 2014. He Left Planet Earth with secrets of life remaining embedded]

GANIT OF *PRAAN SHAKTI?*

The term *ganit* is used in an algorithmic sense - for a systematic understanding of any phenomenon. No mathematical model of Life Force is known yet. The term Life Energy/Force is identified with *praan or praan shakti*. Hindus, in particular, believe in various forms of cultivated powers – like, in the Yoga, different *siddhis* (attained mystical powers) and *kundalini* (ultimate awakening of dormant powers within). The main objective of the paper is to bring this subject into an open forum where some scientific principles can be applied. Limited attempts have been made in the West to understand the effect of meditation and yoga *aasans* (postures) on human body and brain. However, Indian scholars have not yet openly raised this question in academic settings.

The major principles of science are demonstrability or outcome measurements under identical conditions, and statistical hypothesis testing. **The author theorizes that any thing that can be actualized, or self-realized, can be eventually mathematized.** Therefore, a fundamental question is to establish some axioms of *praan shakti*. Once mathematization or a mathematical model of a problem is set up, then one can go from a Point A to a Point B in a progressive, and yet undisputed manner.

In every society and age, people have believed in spiritual powers under various labels and descriptions. Recently, the West has also openly started talking about the healing powers in prayers. A daily life of the Hindus is highly influenced by the good powers of blessings (*aashirvad*) and evil powers of curses *(shaap or shraaps)* etc. The scenario is quite common and witnessed in the Eastern and Latin American societies. Of course, the native Indians of North America and indigenous tribes of Africa continue to practice the healing power of spiritual science under the names like, medicine men or *shamans*.

This paper also raises some salient points including scientific explanation of the raised right hand in parabolic postures of blessings, touching of the feet of a spiritual master, and the power of certain Vedic *mantras* in their recitations. In the context of Life Energy/

Force, some aspects from the lives of recent spiritual masters – like, Ramkrishna Paramahansa, Raman Maharishi and Swami Vivekananda and Swami Dayanand, are discussed.

June 8, 1999/May, 2014

PS: 05/22/2014

The above text is essentially an abstract of a paper presented at the biennial Vedanta conference held on the campus of Osmania University, Hyderabad in August, 1999. The paper is strangely untraceable in the Word files searched so far. However, the text above points out a general mathematical modeling problem in an esoteric domain.

BENJAMIN FRANKLIN & MATH

"....Thomas Godfrey, a self-taught Mathematician, great in his Way, & afterwards Inventor of what is now called Hadley's Quadrant. But he knew little out of his way, and was not a pleasing Companion, as like most Great Mathematicians I have met with, he expected unusual Precision in every thing said, or was forever denying or distinguishing upon Trifles, to the Disturbance of all Conversation. He soon left us...........William Parsons, bred a Shoemaker, but loving Reading, had acquired a considerable Share of Mathematics, which he first studied with a View to Astrology that he afterwards laughed at. He also became Surveyor General."

These excerpts are taken from pp 82-84 of the *Autobiography* of the great American founder, Benjamin Franklin (1706-1790). He gave thumbnail sketches of 10 charter members of the club/junto that he initiated at the age of 20. It was like a **super toastmasters club,** as it also laid emphasis on reading and writing besides public speaking. Combined with the printing press and a newspaper that Franklin owned by the age of 24, the club met every Friday and flourished for several decades. Its opinions and positions on public issues greatly influenced the social and political life of the emerging nation.

I paused after reading these lines, smiled and pondered over. The amazing point is that in the 17th century, popularity of mathematics in the colonies had come to a point that a shoemaker enjoyed teaching it himself! It reminds me of the 16th century saint Raydas, the Guru of famous Krishna devotee, Mirabai, Raydas was also a shoemaker by trade! Art, poetry and music do transcend social stratification, but science and mathematics are entirely different intellectual activities, as they require collaboration and succession for their progress.

In England, 17th century was a golden dawn of mathematics and sciences, as Newton's scientific discoveries had brought a paradigm shift. The intellectuals who formed a vast majority of the early settlers in New England had come from Cambridge with high priority on education. It is similar to the first generation of immigrants coming to the US from India in the 1950s through '70's, who were all professionals. In terms of the impact, the big difference is that the religious persecution of the Protestants in England united them in New England. However, Indians, the Hindus in particular, have remained outside the political mainstream of the USA. Adversities are never welcomed, but they do have a long-term positive effect!

Immediately after the settlers arrived in New England, colleges like Harvard (1636), Yale (1701), Brown (1764) and Dartmouth (1770) were opened up with a mission of service to the church and new territory. With a combination of perfect transplantation and burning enthusiasm, science, math and literature simply exploded in these colonies.

During 1724-25, Benjamin had an 'adventurous' visit to England for 18 months. His biggest disappointment was not being able meet Newton (1642-1727)! Newton, at that time, being the Master of the Royal Mint, old, and in ill health, was perhaps not publicly accessible despite an intermediary that Franklin had approached. Anyway, my simple question is: **how many young people today are eager to go and meet the Nobel Prize Winners or Field Medalists**? Ours is an age of 'who cares', 'me, me, me', and 'If I don't toot my horn, then who else will?'

Being one of the 17 kids of a waxier, Franklin started Grammar School in Boston at age, 8. After two years, he went to a private **School of Writing & Arithmetick**. He was pretty good in writing, "but I failed in Arithmetic & made no progress in it". He was taken out of school at 10 to help in father's business. Later on, at 16, he went back: "…… And now it was that being on some **Occasion made ashamed of my Ignorance in Figures**, which I had failed twice in learning when at school, I took Cocker's Book of Arithmetick, & went through' the whole by myself with great Ease. I also read Seller's & Sturmy's Books of Navigation & became acquainted with the little Geometry they contain, but never proceeded far in that Science…" That is how Benjamin recalled his life and times 50 years later!

Franklin was a voracious reader. In lifetime, he spent more money on books than on his food! Actually, he ate sparingly, but read and wrote with a passion that included science. **"I think no other subject gives a person as much self-confidence as does mathematics when it is self-taught."** On this note, my only absolutely independent learning experience is of special and general theory of relativity studied in the fall of 1961!

Coming back to the quotes and excerpts, Franklin wrote them while on a visit to England in 1772 for three weeks. It is a letter to his son and started at the regular insistence of his friends, who knew the future merits of his autobiography. Franklin, being a very busy public figure and inventor, had no time for extended sittings needed to write a book. This so-called autobiography is a collection of his four-part letters and notes published, as a 200-page memoir after his death. **It is acclaimed as the most widely read autobiography in the US!**

Franklin, being a well-known public figure by the age of 65, must have met quite a few intellectuals including scientists (himself being a great inventor) and mathematicians justifying his general comments on the characteristics of mathematicians. Few will dispute it. **It is an invariant subspace of human psychology.** The demands on exactness, perfection, rigor in solving problems or proving theorem define the nature of mathematics. Eventually, it has to rub off on the deeper psyche of the mathematicians. The strong disagreements between economists are at gross level, but amongst mathematicians, the differences go deep at personal level. It is an extension of $\varepsilon - \delta$ approach in doing mathematics! Whereas, it brings luster to mathematics, but dampens mathematicians in their social settings.

For a little clarification, it is important to add a word or two on the book and its text. Franklin wrote it in parts, when he was 65, 78, and in his 80's. The autobiography that I read it is a 1951 publication of **The Heritage Press**. It is interesting to look at the English language prevalent 300 years ago. Apart from the spellings (for instance 'laught' for 'laughed'), every noun is capitalized and sentences are a mile long with convoluted structure. Nevertheless, it provides a wonderful window at the life of an individual and society that existed 300 years ago. It continues to influence the present!

Jan 20, 2007/Mar 2010

JOB, A JOYOUS JOURNEY

(A Reflective Note to Neal the new Executive VP and Provost)

Yesterday, I read through your interview in the *Inside UNLV*. It was candid; however, your phrases, *"drinking from the fire hose"* and *"running to catch up with trains that have left the stations"*, had me concerned. I hope you are not 'exhausted' like those overheated firefighters and commuters who beat upon the train timings! Being originally from India, the largest network of trains in the world, there are literal dangers. The *Law of Large Numbers* eventually catches up.

Americans work hard with their body and mind. Consequently, they get out of touch with their own spirits. For balancing up the life, medication and meditation are both resorted to in proportionate measures. As a matter of fact, the American work ethics are America's main export to the world, particularly to the sleeping nations like India and China.

Amongst many things that you may have familiarized yourself about the student body, here is my **pop quiz** for you on *UNLV Orientation 101*. It is related with *Elementary Calculus I* (**MATH 181**) that I just finished teaching during summer session III. Generally, freshmen take it in the very first semester. *Elementary Calculus* **defines an institution** in terms of its student quality, FTE (Full Time Equivalent) generated, head count, faculty involvement, and much more. Also, the College Dean has identified MATH 181 as one of the four courses - one from each department – except, Geosciences, for special attention in fall. Here are the following questions in the context of *Elementary Calculus I* (Math 181). Just put your answers down across them. Good luck; it is fun time!

1. Ratio of males and females?
2. Percentage of 18-year olds?
3. The age of the oldest student?
4. Percentage of freshmen?
5. Percentage of sophomores?
6. Percentage of working (part/full)?

7. Percentage of repeaters (including twice or thrice)?
8. Percentage of math majors?
9. Percentage of physics majors?
10. Percentage of bio, chem, comp science, and all engineers combined?
11. Retention rate?
12. Cumulative class GPA?
13. Student Evaluation of my instruction?
14. Profile of the Top Student?

You are welcome to communicate it with anyone around you. It takes new comers a few years for UNLV's perception to gel. The faculty members eventually re-orientate their compasses, but the administrators move on to new pastures.

Finally, check your answers with the specific ones: 1 (55 : 45), 2 (02.5), 3 (47; 3 over 40), 4 (12.5), 5 (20), 6 (60), 7 (50), 8 (00), 9 (00), 10 (58), 11 (80), 12 (2.05/4.0), 13 (2.43/4.0), 14 (freshmen, in 30's, married, father of 2 kids; 10 & 7; wife in the 3rd year of Touro's DO/Doctor of Osteopathic program!).

Aug 24, 2007/July, 2014

PRAYERS AND RESEARCH

A week ago, stepping out of a social club in Malaysia, Said asked me to wait till he finishes his prayer. When he came out within 7-8 minutes, I said, **"Five prayers a day means that a Muslim doesn't have a block of more than 3-4 hours to immerse his/her body and mind into an activity. Doesn't it handicap the devout Muslims to carry out the deeper tasks?"** Elaborating it, I added that several times, my *Reflections* go over 4-5 hours non-stop. With eyes on prayer timings, one cannot effectively tackle research problems.

Said Abubakar, known since my first Malaysian assignment in 1992, is a retired British Airline executive. Now, he finds more time for his neighborhood mosque, Quranic studies and pilgrimages to Mecca and Madina. Having studied in London, he has an open and analytical mind too. We kind of agreed - that by and large, the prayer interruptions may not be consequential in the mundane chores. However, when it comes to engaging the mind in creative works - like expected for winning the Nobel Prizes, there is bound to be a negative impact. Actually, the number of Muslim Nobel Prize winners, in sciences in particular, is relatively insignificant.

This is the first time I posed this question to a Muslim friend, though it propped up in my mind a year ago while teaching a course on *History of Mathematics* (MAT 714). In the class, a correlation between mathematics and organized religions was investigated. A prayer in eastern religions, Hinduism in particular, can be totally personal. Varied assembly prayers are held in ceremonial functions. In Western religions, Islam in particular, prayer, being one of its five pillars, is a communal activity, highly ordained and structured ritual. A Muslim supposedly earns 23 times prayer merit points when it is done in a group. That explains how years ago, while waiting for a train, I was invited by a Muslim traveler to join him in a noon prayer at the Delhi railway platform.

Prayer is one word, but its prescriptions and the images of its worshippers are infinite. An individual person, in a prayer mode, may project an aura of harmony, peace, tranquility and contentment.

However, the collective image of praying persons may send a message of discipline, order, strength and unity. It is reported that of all the religious groups, the Muslims have the highest rate of completing the basic training courses of the US Army.

Generally, prayer is perceived as a means and a bridge for helping an individual in making a connection with his/her Supreme. The medium may include rosaries, prayer beads, mantras, recitation of certain passages from the Holy Books. Yet, great spiritual minds are known to have taken this highroad without any external aid. They can transform any mundane activity into a prayer! That is the height of individual enlightenment and perfection.

I remain curious to see statistical connections between mathematical achievements and religious affiliations. Certain areas of pure mathematics are very abstract and any seminal breakthroughs require days of mental tussle and engagement. Specifically, it would be interesting to collect or find data on the impact of structured and unstructured prayers on the mathematical achievements of groups based on faith and national origin etc.

Jan 09, 2008/July, 2014

A QUESTION THAT BAFFLES ME

(A note to interested mathematical students)

Today's e-mail, forwarded by the Dept. Chair, came down the line of authority - from a university system office. It prompted me to participate in the undergraduate research program, but with only **one** student.

Lately, my expanding mathematical interest has been intersecting with history, anthropology, archaeology, sociology, psychology, and even religion. One of the research problems is in an area of women and mathematics. It sounds as if the presence of women causes some problems for mathematics, or conversely. Not, at all! In fact, the **Association of Women in Mathematics** (AWM) has been promoting and recognizing women in mathematics for decades.

A common scenario in teaching is that the presence of women gets thinner as the level of mathematics goes up. **Does it mean that women are less capable for higher mathematics?** Not at all! Based on my 30-year data, women out-perform men by at least one letter grade in all 100/200 - level lower division math courses. It has been informally corroborated by many other sources. Where is the beef then?

The research problem is on the investigation of the reasons as to why women who are good students in lower division math courses do not continue with mathematics at the upper division and graduate levels. When it comes to necessary data collection, the focus will be on UNLV, as it celebrates its 50th anniversary.

Also, is this a typical American cultural problem, or there is an element of universality about it? It may involve the study of literature of other cultures and nations depending on time. Over all, the investigation will involve the study of literature, collecting data, and analysis. I think the final project report should be interesting to everyone and revealing.

Summer is indeed a good time for such a project. The student will get credits under MATH 499 (**Independent Study**). As far as the number of credits (1-3) is concerned, it will depend upon the time, effort and energy put in.

Feel free to discuss it with me before submitting an application according to the guidelines specified. If there are more than one interested student, then there may be some screening. This is the first time that I am offering this opportunity. I am excited about learning more about this problem through this collaboration. The deadline is March 01.

The eligibility for this program is wide open when it comes to student's major. This problem may also be of interest to students outside mathematics - including sciences, engineering, math education, and more. So feel free to share it with friends and classmates, who may be interested in this academic adventure. It could be like a good summer hike in the mountains!

My office is CBC/B410; phone number, 895-0383; E-mail: bhatnaga@ unlv.nevada.edu .

Jan 30, 2008

COMMENTS

You should obtain the following book on this subject:

Women and Mathematics: Balancing the Equation by Susan F. Chipman (Editor), Lorelei R. Brush (Editor), Donna M. Wilson (Editor)

Studies have been carried out by SRI and Peabody Institute on this topic. You can review their findings.—**Avnish**

Dr. B- I think that the picture is clouded by the issue of career versus family. In the 122/123 classes I most often teach, women outnumber men by 8 or 10 to 1. A teaching credential is something that a girl can use almost anywhere-------and there is less commitment involved, i.e., less possible interference with future marriage and family options than there would be if a girl becomes highly qualified in a field such as statistics. Traditionally, the wife subordinates her job to the husband's job, and a wife with high-level credentials in math is less free to adjust her career to that of a husband than she would be if she were certified as a teacher. **Owen Nelson**

PERSONAL REMARKS

MATHEMATICS IN SUPER BOWL

Last Thursday, I announced an extra credit assignment in all my classes. *'Write a 500-word report relating mathematics with Super Bowl including its media fanfare.'* Learning is also making far-fetched connections. Encouragingly, I told that mathematics might be found in 101 scenarios. Staying thoughtful and vigilant all the time are the keys whether one is engrossed in the game or not. Of course, I added that I would also work on this assignment, and share it with them at the next meeting.

Being in the profession for many years, it wasn't difficult for me to enjoy the excitement of Super Bowl while keeping an eye for mathematics submerged in it. After nearly 50 years of collegiate teaching, mathematics has become a paradigm and window of my life. It is easier to get a point when it has mathematical flavor. I am not taking an extreme position that eventually every thing is reducible to bare mathematics. The derivation needs to be within the grasp of the undergraduate students. That is a boundary condition. Any ways, here are three types of my super bowl inspired mathematical observations:

Surface Mathematics is seen in the odds over 200 different kinds of bets. The initial spread of 14 points was posted after statistical analyses of a mound of data on previous games, records, player injuries and playing conditions etc. It involves mathematical probability and statistical inference. Its elements are also taught in MATH 132 (Finite Mathematics) and STAT 152 (Introduction to Statistics). Amongst the bets, the one that was easy to beat or win was the odds on a tie game when the spread remained at least 12. The casinos move the betting lines with the money coming in. It is cold counting - monitored every second.

I admire the odd makers as intuitive combinatorians. The Super Bowl spread was announced within seconds of the end of the second conference championship game played two weeks earlier. The Las Vegas casinos are set to rake in $100 millions. Again, a 'linear' projection on the data of the intakes of the last 4-5 years gives a good estimate. Most graphic calculators have it.

Shallow Mathematics is seen, say, behind the sorting routines applied on every conceivable record category. The sorting algorithms are introduced in upper division computer science courses. I got a kick when the commentator announced that three points scored in the first quarter were the lowest in a Super Bowl. That was right on my mind when it was announced. Inputting the data and getting instantaneous output is a marvel of mathematics behind the programming codes. Random search of data from a bank is a hot research area.

Deep Mathematics lies behind nano technology, entertainment engineering, and communication through compressed videos. One instance is QB Brady's gadget on his left forearm for checking the plays sent from the sidelines. There is mathematics of trajectories when QB Manning shot and lobbed for touchdowns. They are 'mathematically' perfected during drills and in strength rooms. I am not underestimating the role of psychology, as there is no rehearsal for Super Bowl distracting hoopla.

Whereas, Super Bowl is the largest symphony in the US, men and technologies behind the scene capture mathematical precision in their coordination. For instance, assembling and dis-assembling of the huge stage in the middle of the playfield for halftime entertainment takes place in seconds. The proof that **Time is Money** is seen in a price tag of $ 2.7 million for a 30-second advertisement!

Feb 04, 2008/July, 2014

A MATHEMATICAL TOUCH

Last Sunday, I attended a lecture at the joint meeting of the *Humanistic (Atheistic) Society* and the *Society of Rational Thoughts*. The atheists have a national organization, but the *Rational Thoughts* is local. Once I told an avowed atheist, "You're an ultimate theist!" Man (generic use) is born free of conditionings; an hypothesis; *Believe It Or Not* (BION). Gradually, man turns into a theist, believer in say, a super power, at some point in life, and later on, rejecting a notion of god, turns into an atheist, and so on. BION.

I no longer engage myself in the discussions between atheists and theists, as it seems scoring points without clear agreement on the basic premises. It is like 'playing' a game without consensus on any rules. This realization dawned on me due to mathematical enlightenment after 40 years in the 'business' at the macro level, not micro. BION

Rob, the President of the *Society of Rational Thoughts* recognized me at the meeting. He was my non-traditional Honors student 20 years ago! He also impressed me by recalling 'calculus' moments. Well, I surprised him too by recalling his driving to the Campus from Pahrump, 55 miles away. As a side bar, prostitution is legal in Pahrump, in Nye County. It is not legal in Clark County, where Las Vegas is located. That alone throws rational thoughts out of the window, and so goes the humanistic, theist, or atheist corollaries.

Anyway, at the end of the talk, I surmised, "*Atheist* $= \lim_{n \to \infty} (Theist)^n$." Rob was so excited about it that he wanted to have it printed on t-shirts. That prompted me to refine my 'mathematical' show-off. Here is a crude set-theoretic model to ponder upon.

Universal Set, U of all human beings who believe in demonstrable or non-demonstrable beliefs. Demonstrable means like scientific experiments or mathematical proofs. U is not the entire human race as little kids do not even understand what 'believing' is! BION.

Religion R_n is set of human beings who profess n non-demonstrable beliefs. Religion is used in a **generic** sense. It also includes organized religions, cults, and creeds etc.

Complement, R_n^c is the set of persons repudiating the n beliefs of believers in R_n.

Union, $R_i \cup R_j$ is the set of people having every belief of R_i or (inclusive **or**) R_j. It is reasonable to assume that $R_i \perp R_j$, if $i \neq j$. It means there is at least one belief that is **not common** between any two religions. However, it is possible that the intersection, R_i and R_j may be an empty set, ϕ, for some $i \neq j$. $R_n \neq \phi$ *for all n.* **It is all at time, t.**

A set of atheists (Not clearly well defined), A $= \left(\lim_{\substack{n \to \infty}} \bigcup_{k=1}^{n} R_n \right)^c$. **Conjecture:** A is empty.

Remarks: 1. At any time t, an atheist believes in at least one non-demonstrable belief.
2. No one is an atheist or theist for all time t that is for his/her entire life span. BION!

Mar 22, 2008/July, 2014

COMMENTS

Interesting. However, I think the definition can't distinguish an atheist from someone who believes in a <u>negative theology</u>. Like Bulla, for instance. Best, **Anil** (Menon)

I wrote: There is a Hindu philosophical/theological thought, called *Naiti Naiti* means *'this is not, this is not'*. That is a problem in defining an atheist. The list of 'this is not' cannot be exhausted. It is like trying to define a healthy person who does not have this health problem, this problem, and this problem, and it goes on.

Dear Satish: Thanks for your communication. Jesus was a Theist. For him, theist meant one who believes in the Creator of all as in Genesis 1:1. The Bible reveals that the Creator exists. Modern science is coming to that conclusion, as I have discovered. **Varughese**

Bhai Sahib, thanks for sending me your reflections. I read most of them but this "Mathematical touch" goes above my brain. Any way I do not have to know every mathematical formula. At this stage, I forget my entire math, as I have never used after my BS in Electrical from Bhopal University in 1973. Regards. **Pramod!**

PARADIGM SHIFTS

I watched Wimbledon Tennis for the Williams sisters. They were the biggest draw of the tournament, as they steamrolled through their single and double matches. During the all-sister single final, I observed that the Williams sisters and their parents, who as co-coaches have brought a paradigm, shift in women's tennis. The sisters did not go to an elite tennis academy, or attend elite colleges on tennis scholarships. They were totally street raised and home grown. It is their incredible training regimen, on the top of genetic physique, that they stand out as thoroughbred tennis players.

Taking this paradigm shift as an exercise, I thought of making a list of paradigm shifts in other aspects of life too. Though I am only a sport aficionado, here are a few more to get it going:

Boxing (Heavyweight); Muhammad Ali's **Rope a Dope,** fight with the 'invincible' George Foreman (1974). The genius of Ali that even baffled his trainer, who was sitting at the ringside.

Basketball: Michael Jordon's will to win and never to wilt in a game set new benchmarks. He was coached by legends - in the college by Dean Smith and by Phil Jackson with Chicago Bulls.

Golf: Tiger Woods trained by his father. Incidentally, Tiger chose Stanford over UNLV for Golf. His father predicted Tiger's phenomenal success in a book, but the golf professionals did not believe him.

Mathematics: Invention of **Calculus** by Newton and Leibnitz changed the face of mathematics and sciences. One of the many ways to describe Calculus is the **Taming of Infinity**. Come to think of another mathematical invention during the last 100-200 years, nothing else stands out in my mind except both abstraction and applications of mathematics reaching newer heights. Mathematical rigor got another push in 1945 from Bourbaki - a group of French mathematicians. Incidentally, the French, Augustine Cauchy (1789-1857) had given the first push.

Physics: Special and General Theory of Relativity. It has brought far-reaching consequences due to the study of high speeds near that of light, subatomic particles, and birth of nano-science. The traditional walls in sciences, of physics, chemistry, and biology, are falling down.

The **inventions** like airplanes, automobiles, spacecrafts and personal computers have also changed the courses of mankind. The latest cellular technology has brought internet, video and audio in the palm of a hand. While the geographic distances are eliminated, a person, now increasingly confined in the privacy of his/her own 'island', has become far more vulnerable.

July 4, the US Independence Day, and Wimbledon have converged. I venture to say **that of all nations born or created in history, the USA today is an example of a paradigm shift**. The US went unnoticed for the first 125 years – like, the Williams sisters' début 15 years ago. They were also ridiculed for braiding white beads into their hairdos and dresses they designed. Their father was not given any credit for the book he wrote on their tennis training. But the sisters kept wining, and wining so big time, that Chris Evert, a woman-tennis legend of the 1970s, recently said, "The Williams sisters are too strong to play with women!" The rest is history.

July 06, 2008/July, 2014

PS: 07/07/2014 - This thought started from tennis to math and to whatever came across my mind. However, it is a worthy exercise to be shared with the students to stimulate their minds. A few years ago, when I posed this question to a dentist, his prompt reply was dental implants – a paradigm shift in dentistry.

A MATHEMATICAL CONFERENCE

Professional workshops, meetings and conferences provide opportunities for continuing education, exchange of ideas and research collaboration. Also, one can network with various professionals, and visit new places. Some how, I only started attending them from the 1980s. Now attending at least one meeting a year is a must. During early years, the purpose was 75% professional, and 25% social and cultural. These percentages have been reversing lately. Conferences are places to arm wrestle with ideas on 1-1, 1-many and many-1 bases. With mind over matter, it is pertinent to stay mentally sharp in later years of life.

During Dec 19-21, 2008, I was an invited speaker at a national conference of the Society for the History of Mathematics. Its role in science and society was the conference theme. The venue was the campus of Manipur University (MU), Imphal, recently upgraded to one of the sixteen central universities of India. Upgrading the status means more money than a university needs. As a result, universities in India agitating for upgrades have turned it into political issues. This situation is in sharp contrast with the US state and private universities, which are facing severe budgets cuts due to tsunami economic downturns.

With so many large construction projects underway at MU, one of the hosts remarked that the MU can't spend the allocated money fast enough. For millennia, India has been a land of extremes in riches and poverty – both at the individual and institutional levels. Yet, no French or Russian Revolution is ever going to take place in India!

Imphal is the capital of Manipur, an easternmost state of India with border common with Myanmar (Burma). For a number of reasons, it is not easily accessible by road, train or air. This geographical isolation has been a part of its recent history due to political turmoil going on in entire eastern India. Otherwise, Manipur legends have been the fabrics of Indian folklores since eons in *Ramayana* and *Mahabharata*.

Consequently, only a dozen Indian participants came from outside Manipur. Most papers were presented by the faculty from MU and from nearby affiliated colleges in Manipur. From the opening remarks of the Vice-Chancellor (equivalent to president of a US university) it was obvious that this conference had put MU on a research map of India. Sometimes, parochial mindsets gradually change with intellectual investments in new centers.

I was the sole foreign invitee to make it to Imphal despite repeated e-mails warnings by the US State Department after the first, Oct 30, serial bomb blasts in Guwahati, the capital city of Assam state. That was right, as the second serial bombings exploded on New Year Day of 2009! Life is all about beating the odds, and Las Vegas, my hometown in the US, thrives on this outlook in life.

However, this conference gave me much more than professional satisfaction. Now I can 'boast' of having touched all the four extremities of India; Kanyakumari in south (1986), Jaiselmer in west (1987), Amarnath in north (1998), and Imphal (2008) in east. Such unplanned experiences measure a quality of life on its own plane.

The Conference received generous support from MU and two central agencies. The registration fees of all the invited speakers were defrayed. In fact, Indian invited speakers were reimbursed huge travel expenses. The board and lodging were taken care by MU through University Guest House conveniently located. At times, I would think how at University of Nevada Las Vegas (UNLV), a typical US university, faculty members scurry around for financial support from their departments and travel committees. In contrast, during the last 8-10 years, faculty travel support in India has greatly improved.

However, Americans have perfected a successful formula for organizing conferences of any sizes. Bigger the better, is an American way to draw the numbers. For instance, the Joint Annual Meeting of 5-7 US mathematics organizations is the grandest show on earth - drawing over 5000 mathematicians. It is held every January attracting mathematics professional and students from more than 100 countries.

The Society for History of Mathematics, based in Delhi University, is perhaps one of the 20 independent mathematics organizations in India. For instance, Indian Mathematical Society is more than 100 years old, but its annual meetings, held every December, draw hardly 100 local and outside attendees. The number of math faculty, in nearly 5000 Indian colleges and universities, may be at least 30,000. Yet, they are not even partly together. **Mathematics flourishes with organization**.

There is another dimension to this scenario. Indian mathematics organizations, like most other Indian institutions, are driven by personalities rather than by larger institutional missions. As a matter of fact, they reflect the individualism and diversity in Hinduism, the major religion of the land. "Has there been an effort to have a joint meeting of a few, if not all, mathematics organizations?" "Never!" responded an officer of the Society.

Interestingly enough, most papers presented were not all related with history of mathematics. I heard it said, that out of nearly 400 papers received, only 76 were accepted and their abstracts published. Yet, hardy 30 dealt with history, and fewer were close to the theme of the conference. One idea to promote research culture in a remote part of the country is by paper presentations. Therefore, most papers were on hard-core analysis, fuzzy sets, number theory, statistics, topology, computer algorithms, fractals, physics, and biology. A bottom line is that every conference needs warm bodies.

A few papers beat around Vedic Mathematics encrypted in ancient scriptures like the Vedas and Upvedas. The scholars knowing mathematics, and Vedic Sanskrit and grammar have not existed in India for at least 200 years. Moreover, they are not likely to come out of any present Indian college or university for another 100 years. It is all due to archaic curriculum history of India. Such papers are superficial and lack in depth. Any research nugget, dug from deep past, needs to be connected with present for better future.

In the US, the sessions on history of mathematics, at national or sectional meetings, are most popular. The MAA has a special interest group on it. The main reason is that the history of world mathematics, since the 15th century, is simply the history of European mathematics. **Hindu mathematicians, ruled by foreigners since 11th century, lived in anonymity, or in the shadows of their protectors**. Lot of open research questions are there on their lives and works in each century since the 6th century - the golden period of India.

There is an element of universality about history of mathematics. Like in the US, invitees and presenters have traditional doctorates in mathematics. In fact, I am not aware of any university awarding PhD in History of Mathematics. More than half the officers of the Society are retired mathematics professors. I often inquire how they developed interest in history of mathematics. Generally, it is evolutionary in nature. Also, it is a corollary of GH Hardy's theory, that hard-core math problems cannot be cracked without teeth or even with dentures. History of mathematics phases in, as typical mathematics phases out, say after the age of 50.

My interest in history of mathematics is a corollary of my interest in world history. During the last 25 years, I have designed courses, taught undergraduate and graduate courses, and presented papers on history of mathematics. In addition, several *Mathematical Reflections* have been written on the subject.

This conference turned out to be the smallest national conference ever attended. On a positive side note, lot of interaction with a few participants occurred in informal gatherings. It was partly due to the fact, that we were confined to the MU campus. Armed units were deployed every 100' off campus including country sides.

Despite abnormal political conditions, one evening, we were exclusively treated to famous Manipuri music and dances. On the last day, 5-6 hours were spent in sightseeing Moirang area, 40 KM from Imphal. It is famous for historic Indian National Army Museum, and a huge lake that has man-made floating islands.

It was all a part of MU hospitality—unthinkable in the US culture, where you pay for everything. Nevertheless, nothing is free in life either. In India, taxpayers foot the bills. Transportation was available for shopping for the spouses who came along and guest pick-up/drop-off at Imphal Airport! At the airport, a few of us were presented one KG of red rice, Manipur is famous for. That was an icing on the cake.

Putting every thing together, it made this conference a memorable experience.

Jan 03, 2009/July 2014

PERSONAL REMARKS

MATH STUDENTS AT THE UN

I arrived at the University of Nizwa (UN) Campus on Jan 17, 2009; a week before the classes started on Jan 24. I was prepared for my new job in a new culture. The first week turned out to be unforgettable, as out of the eight classes only one met with only one student. It never happens in a US university. Let me tell you at the outset, that the UN is modeled after a US university - both in its degree programs and administrative structures. As a matter of fact, some course descriptions are nearly identical to the ones offered at the University of Nevada Las Vegas (UNLV), I am associated with since 1974.

The second week was no better either. Apart from staggered attendance, the textbook distribution delayed instruction in right spirits. In fact, a couple of students collected their textbooks in the third week! At UNLV, the students buy their own textbooks online or from the bookstores before the classes begin. The textbooks are posted online a month in advance. Some students get head starts on the courses before classes begin. What a contrast!

I never thought of book distribution chores; its paper work - getting the books from a warehouse and keeping track of books. The recordkeeping made me nervous a few times. I told my students to lessen my anxiety by returning the books on the days of the Final Exams. I would go back to the US right after the exams. Otherwise, the I-grades may not be removed!

It makes me wonder, how you can develop respect for scholarship, if you don't have the books. Respect for books lies in buying them, studying them and referring to them off and on. It is mind boggling that students get bachelor's degrees without owning a single textbook. As history buff, let me tell you that several times in Middle East, many libraries, including that of Alexandria, the largest in the world at one time, were burnt away. There may be some historical connection between books and scholarship.

Going back to my trail of thought, don't get me wrong. I am not counting my days of leaving Oman. I came with my choice to see people, their customs and traditions. You can never get it all by reading or watching the videos. **You don't understand mathematics either by reading examples or watching others do it!**

When I noticed all girls and only one boy in all three courses, I told a colleague that these girls must be very good at mathematics. In 40 years of teaching in India, Malaysia and the US, the average grade of the girls is at least one grade higher than that of the boys. But the UN girls may provide a counter example, though there is only one male student!

I told the students that I have come here to learn from you – the Omani people, culture and monuments. Teaching is the only profession I have done since 1961; my first professional love, and hopefully the last. Lately, I have started fluttering my wings as a writer too. My style of instruction is not with my back towards the students, but rather engaging them in eye-to-eye manner at every step of the way, when problems are discussed. The goal is to open a window of mind to the beauty of *Mathematical Thinking* based on *deductive reasoning*; not cold memorization!

Feb 23, 2009/Jan 10, 2010

WAL-MART, JMM & KUMBH

I really have fun attending the annual Joint Mathematics Meetings (JMM), as I do, at times, shopping in the Wal-Mart Super Centers. Under one Wal-Mart roof, one can buy any household product and service, furthermore, at a price that is not easily beaten. That is how I told a colleague when we ran into each other at the JMM - outside a restroom servicing dozens of people at a time. The 2010 meeting (January 13-16) was held in a three-storey humongous Mascone Center-West - right in the heart of San Francisco. Marriot Hotel across the Mascone Center also had some meeting rooms. With 50' glass walls in silvery steel frames on three sides, it provided panoramic views of inside-out and outside-in.

Nearly 5800 persons were registered and 1900 papers and invited talks were presented. The JMM provides the ultimate mathematics buffet - including mathematical soups, salads, disserts, appetizers on the top of ethnic bites, tacos, burritos, enchiladas, and name Chinese wok frieds. There is closeness when it comes to eating and soaking mathematical ideas. Both are primed for the young at head and heart. At 20, I recall my appetite - once cleaning up, on a bet, two pounds of ground meat with rice. With equal ferocity, books and knowledge were devoured. Sometimes, at 70, I feel a mere shadow of myself in both of these pursuits. The only edge that I have over my 20s is in my ability of bridging diverse ideas. It was not possible in my youth. The accumulated data and knowledge often burst out in braided forms.

The next day, after soaking in some lectures and having done with my paper presentation, as I was relaxing with a drink, it occurred to me that the JMM is like Hindu *Kumbh Mela*, held in India. *Kumbh* means pitcher and *mela* means fair. In millennia old Hindu mythology, *Kumbh* symbolizes a Pitcher of Perfect Knowledge to be shared with the seekers. *Kumbh Melas* are held in a lunar month in four places - Prayag, Ujjain, Nasik, Haridwar, in different 12-year cycles. Each site also hosts a 6-year half *Kumbh Mela*. It is the ultimate place to share, demonstrate and watch the newest results in harnessing spiritual energies at the individual levels. Yes, whereas, mathematics is the most organized knowledge and thrives on collaboration, but spiritual 'mathematics' is eventually one-man journey. There are no multiple authorships in this endeavor.

The Hindus, in millions, converge to the **Kumbh** site for an ultimate spiritual buffet by visiting the scantily clad spiritual masters, sadhus, and sanyasis of different religious orders. They are like modern scholars holding different degrees and diplomas. The masses often imbibe spiritual vibrations by seating themselves as close as possible to the masters. It is the oldest tradition of Hindu way of life and learning at the deepest levels. Incidentally, Haridwar is currently hosting a 12-year **Kumbh Mela**. The dates of the **Kumbh Melas** are flexible in an open interval over a lunar month. They are not defined like the dates of the JMM, which are in a close interval.

I have yet to witness a **Kumbh mela**. Reading and watching videos about the **Kumbh** won't capture the sounds, smells, sights within sights and soulful magical touches. Like a couple of hundred exhibitors at the JMM, a **Kumbh mela** draws thousands of vendors selling everything from amulets to jewelry. It is a place where indigenous drugs and intoxicants are openly indulged in and tolerated. After all, what are stronger - modern laws or the ageless traditions? At the JMM, it is most common to go out for drinks during lunches and dinners. After all, the best ideas are often thrashed and sorted over drinks and smokes.

In the world of mathematics too, the seminal theorems are not proved every year - but every few years. The annual JMM captures the young and encourages them at early stages. Both the **Kumbh** and JMM lure the young and restless minds to their folds. The JMM provides forums to all sorts of math sub-groups and affiliations like alumni of many universities. The Association of Christians in Mathematical Sciences had their own banquet. Victor Katz offered a course on Mathematics of Islam. I see a strong correlation between mathematics and theology. Of course, the Vedic Mathematics of ancient India is now so well known worldwide.

At the **Kumbh Mela**, the most revered group of yogic masters live in total nudity with holy ashes smeared over the bodies. I am told that these are the honored ones who inaugurate the *melas* after leading a procession, while the masses are prostrating towards them on either side. Well, at the JMM, it is, perhaps, matched by a reception of the Association of Lesbian, Gay, Bisexual and Transgendered Mathematicians.

The sessions of mathematical poetry, theatrical performance, and knitting stretch the frontiers of mathematics to new horizons. I did not go to any one of them. Hopping over talks and receptions easily constipate me intellectually. We all can digest this much. However, one thing that stands out is that mathematics advances science and technology, and conversely. Having lagged behind in technology, I feel, at times, as if living in a dark cave of electronic age!

Jan 16-31, 2010

A JAMBOREE OF MATHEMATICS

The annual Joint Mathematics Meetings (JMM) is a consortium meeting of six mathematics organizations-AMS (American Mathematical Society), MAA (Mathematical Association of America), SIAM (Society of Industrial and Applied Mathematics), ASL (Association of Symbolic Logic), AWM (Association for Women in Mathematics), and NAM (National Association of Mathematicians), mainly focusing on Afro-Americans. Let it be personalized by adding that the AWM and NAM were incorporated after my migration to the US in 1968. The JMM-2011, held in New Orleans (Jan 06-09, 2011), set records by drawing over 6000 participants and presentations of 2300 talks and papers.

In a whirling crowd, it feels good to be suddenly recognized. On my part, I don't hesitate to say hi to a person known by face, name, or fame. **Human beings are programmed to live for their names**. For the young faculty, job searches and paper presentations are the main reasons of coming to the JMM. I started attending JMM only in late 1980s, since my interest in post-doctoral research had hitherto declined. Being not sure of my new scholarly activities, it was compounded by my 'stage' fear of public speaking. But a good reason was Michael Golberg (1941-2008), a UNLV colleague till 1990. In a *Mathematical Reflections*, I named him, *'An Euler I knew'*. Michael considered attending conferences as wastage of time - taken away from research. His research collaboration was all local.

New Orleans has a touch of Las Vegas, in terms of a huge casino on Mississippi River. Also, there are adult clubs and outlets. The famed Bourbon Street was only two blocks away from the Marriott and Sheraton hotels where the JMM activities were housed. It naturally made me wonder at the 'hypocrisy' of the JMM brass in excluding Las Vegas, since 1971, from holding the JMM. For the last 20 years, I have been waging one-man campaign for bringing the JMM to Las Vegas.

Yesterday's highlight of my stay was an evening walk on the action packed Bourbon Street. There were acrobats, jugglers, close-up magicians and mimes – freely showing their talents. Of course, there were 'strip' girls openly enticing with their hardwares. Men, women and liquor make the most combustible compound in the world. Every eating and musical place had 'three (drinks) for one' signs beating 'two for one' signs in Las Vegas! Naturally, as long as I was on the Bourbon Street, my hand was on the wallet. Today, after breakfast, I enjoyed salubrious River Walk before hitting the intellectual festivities.

The JMM is humungous in every organizational category. Largeness in not always great, but Americans love it large. It is biggest show of mathematicians on earth. One day, the Chinese may beat the Americans, but never Indians. Why? It is an open ethno-mathematics question. Just like my food intake has been getting smaller for the last few years, it applies to my intellectual intake too – but not to the intellectual output! In fact, a **conservation principle applies to what one takes in - it is called, learning - and what one brings out as 'experiential knowledge'**.

This year, I attended only a couple of paper presentations and one keynote address of Keith Devlin to the MAA Special Interest Group, *Philosophy of Mathematics*. The topic was *Will the real philosophy of mathematics please stand up.* He delivered it excellently both in contents and style. I am a charter member of the MAA-SIGPOM.

My missing a session or two was due to a highly touted NFL game between Seattle and New Orleans. I watched it in Sheraton Hotel lounge and bar while drinking beer and typing this *Reflection* on my laptop. The game made its history and so did I, as it was my first football game in a classy bar. I love historical moments in any shape or form. However, in my area of interest, there was only one paper that stimulated my thinking.

Jan 08, 2011

RELATIVITY-SCIENCE-DIVINITY!

Lately, I have been irresistibly drawn towards the astronomy seminars regularly organized by UNLV's Department of Physics and Astronomy. Formally, I never studied astronomy in school or college - nor did it seriously on my own. In fact, I have never peered at the sky through a telescope – though I did buy one for my son when he was in school. Such an opportunity or expense was out of question in Bathinda (India) of the 1950s where I grew up there. In the US, there are all kinds of astronomy clubs of stargazers. However, never any media news, of some midnight 'sparklers' or 'shower' in the sky, would pull me out of the house.

My reasons for attending the colloquiums are **two and a half**! The main reason is of **relativity** - in size. What I mean is - say, compare my body mass of 160 Lbs, which is perhaps 10 to the power 1000 times the mass of a 'non-living' photon or 'living' bacterium (both supposedly of negative masses!). This is one end of a spectrum. Astronomy lectures take one to the other extreme. Yesterday's talk by a Berkeley professor was on **Supernovae**. A supernova is a stellar explosion - more energetic than **Nova**. It is so luminous that 'briefly' it outshines the entire **galaxy**! In a 'short' span, it radiates more energy that a sun would give out in its entire life. The explosion expels much of its matter at a speed that is one tenth of the speed of light.

For putting these popular astronomy objects in perspective, Supernova is explained in terms of a Nova, and Nova is explained in terms of a White Dwarf star! Also, a **galaxy** is a massive (10 billion times of sun!) gravitational bound system that consists of stars and stellar remnants, an interstellar medium of gas and dust, and poorly understood **Dark Matter.** Remember, how the scientists, in 1895, had named the unknown rays, as **X-ray**!

I can say with 'absolute' certainty that the meanings of all these terms are in flux. Yes, stardust is no different from the dust in our home carpets embedded all over! The most familiar astronomically concept, **star**, is defined as a massive luminous ball of plasma held together by gravity. The nearest star from earth is the sun in our planetary system.

Some stars are thousand times that of the sun. All this gives me a real 'high' of some sort. The mathematical definition of **Limit** adds the ultimate salsa to my imagination. My 160 Lbs. mass is literally reduced to zero, or to 'minus' mass in comparison to these truly **astronomical** masses. Yet, the impact of this short 120 Lbs. of Chinese-Berkeley professor is significant - to the extent, that Adam Riess, one of the three 2011- Nobel Prize winners in astrophysics, e-mailed him to compliment him on his recent discovery. He proudly displayed this e-mail in his lecture slide!

There were amusing highlights during the lectures. It was fascinating to know that amateurs discover 20% of the supernovae! It reminds me of some college kids who find the largest primes, graphs of exotic curves in polar coordinates, or results in number theory using the power of parallel computing. It really stopped my thoughts in a track when he mentioned that out of 15,000 galaxies known so far, only 1000 – 3000 are observed during one night. I wanted to know, if any two galaxies are mutually disjoints. Either, I did not make my question clear, or he missed it. Their being distinct means - like 20 golf balls, is just not conceivable to me.

A topper for me, being from the world of mathematics, was of his submitting two research papers in two weeks! I have heard of this 'astronomical' research productivity in a previous colloquium too. In contrast, Andrew Wiles hardly published any research paper for seven years before proving *Fermat's Last Theorem* in 1994!

In a lighter vein, it is said that the substance of an experimental research paper may be shorter than the number of its co-authors including the names of the entire research group, which may be global these days. However, there is one honcho who may take 90% of the credit - like a mafia boss or drug cartel. Man's nature is intrinsically the same – control freak and take-it-all.

When I heard him say that the universe was de-accelerating in 1995, but has been accelerating since 1998, I could not help wondering. What is this – you take research credits for both theories! I was so amused at the models, simulations that are largely the reason of such conclusions. A telescope - like Hubble Space Telescope, does not come out every decade. They are expensive toys - costing in millions of $$. He drew a few laughs when he pointed out a difference in two slides of the same 'sky'. One was taken through a telescope costing 'measly' 2-3 million $$ and other, one billion $$!

For a moment, I was thrown into the utilitarian aspect of all researches in the present state of national economy. A couple of years ago, some UNLV professors in sociology department were doing research on prostitutes and prostitution. A UK sociologist was also collaborating with them. American universities are notorious for doing esoteric research too. A congressional report used to publish trivialization of research.

The **Number Two** is the power of 2-dimensional (2-D) media for explaining a 3-D universe. The dots on the slides represented stars and galaxies! What a power of a point that Euclid defined, and Newton derived his laws of motion of a particle, and it still goes on. We live in 3-D world, but all our digital communications and entertainment are in 2-D - from papers to slides to writing boards.

The talk was not 'hocus-pocus', as it may appear. He kept saying - 'for doing some science'. How can you do science when there is no defined lab, and an experiment, which cannot be duplicated under identical circumstances – the very essence of science? However, I was impressed, when he referred to Chandrasekhar Mass and Chandra Imaging. S. Chandrasekhar (1910-1995) jointly won the 1983-Nobel Prize in astrophysics, but he was highly mathematical. Like Einstein, he saw more of the sky through his equations than through high-powered telescopes.

Now comes the **Reason Number Two and a Half**! While listening to the talks on stars, galaxies, light years etc., I try to read off the astronomers' beliefs in God or its perception. Strangely, it is never revealed! Generally, humans look at the sky, whenever they are awed or wowed by the height of a moment. They don't look down at earth, as how can God be walking at the same level. They don't think of God in the ground, as it is a burial place for dead humans. 'Soul going up' – thus, sky is likely to be the only 'abode' of God. The astronomers are cool, and least interested in God's location! Besides, life in any forms, existing or not, may belong to the domain of astro-biology/ biochemistry/biophysics!

Nonetheless, an hour spent in these colloquia has been always stimulating. The colloquium day and time is set on Friday at 3:30 PM. It is a perfect time for intellectual excursions. Refreshment is served too. A few excited ones continue the discussions in bars across campus – the American way of bonding for projects and research. For a host of reasons, this after-lecture social ritual has bypassed me! For me, it is just enough to ruminate for a little more time.

Oct 22, 2011

COMMENTS

1. It's incomprehensible how someone would have a stimulating mental discussion and use the same tool that they study with (their brain) and hammer at it killing brain cells with alcohol. Some people don't use their education. I watch the PBS show Nova and am tinged with awe over findings that make the television presentation understandable for the layman. But is any of it new? No. It simply is reinterpreted differently.

When in Los Angeles I would attend lectures at the Philosophical Research Institute (among many of my not so popular and avant-garde places I frequented) and would hear presentations on astronomy and relativity and even more so on religion and science. Growing up close to JPL, and fascinated by the mysterious I too asked to be gifted a telescope as a teen and star-gazing became part of my informal education (actually a past time). I grew up going on school field trips to Mt. Baldy to look at the stars. Later I tried to read books written by scientists and couldn't understand any of them.

So, I became fascinated by the Big Bang Theory and turned to novelist Zecharia Sitchen, whose theories on the origins of the human race inhabiting the earth were eye opening. In the end, what I walked away with is this; any profound sort of scientific mind even without a peculiar religious feeling of his own will question man's beginnings.

But it is different from the religion of the naive man. For the latter God is a being from whose care one hopes to benefit and whose punishment one fears; a sublimation of a feeling similar to that of a child for its father.

But the scientist is possessed by the sense of universal causation. The future, to him, is every whit as necessary and determined as the past. His religious feeling takes the form of amazement at the harmony of natural law, which reveals intelligence of superiority, that compared with all the systematic thinking and acting of human beings, is an utterly insignificant reflection. **Linda**

2. Satish, Glad to hear you are getting interested in Astronomy. It is a fascinating field and a real strength at UNLV. Take care. **Len**

3. Wow, there are very interesting musings! Some very deep and thought provoking topics here. Take care, **Tim Porter,** Dean College of Sciences

4. Like you, I've never had formal instruction in astronomy. I've never even looked at stars or planets or the moon with an instrument more powerful than the binoculars I use for bird identification. Growing up on a farm, I was able to see the night sky without interference from street lights, house lights, etc., and I could see the Milky Way and constellations like the Big Dipper. Now, living in the city, I can't see anywhere near the number of stars-----but I at least remember them. I wonder if we don't have young adults who have never seen the night sky in all its glory. They're not only nature-deprived, they're astronomy-deprived.

From a Math Ed point of view, I feel that we need to do much more than we are now doing to develop in our students the ability to comprehend magnitude, whether it be enormous distances like those encountered in astronomy, ultra-long periods of time like those encountered in geology, or tiny distances like those encountered in biochemistry. The ability to comprehend a light year, a petabyte, a nanometer, or a picocurie will never be there without a much better concept of magnitude than we find in our students today, and, if there is any point in our traditional math sequence where we set out to systematically develop such concepts, I am unaware of it.

Everyone should experience now and then an intellectual renewal similar to your experience with astronomy, and many do, quite often by themselves and without formal instruction. I am reminded of something I heard thirty or forty years ago. John Goodland, who was at the time one of the "great thinkers" in the field of K-12 education, was asked how we can tell that a child's intellectual development is sub-standard. His response was that he would not be especially concerned about any child's intellectual development so long as they developed by 8th grade or so a special interest in something where they knew more about it than any of their peers or family. He didn't care if it was dinosaurs, stamps, coins, the guitar, gardening, or robots. I would guess that your current interest in astronomy is not the first "special interest" in your lifetime. **ONN**

A TRUCE WITH A BOOK

In the world of mortals, so far, books alone have survived as my longest companions. There are so many memorable encounters that they may fill an empty book. I literally devoured them in my 20s. Later on, I became selective, as my reading slowed down due to my growing interest in mathematics. Speed reading and math comprehension are opposing activities. In math, if you are not clear about a single step - just one, in a proof of a theorem or solution of a problem, then it is inane to skip it and move on.

My general curiosity remains in 'good' books of any genre. Often, a book is started on the recommendation of a friend, a reviewer of integrity, or its convincing preface. How long a book engages my mind is another story. A good friend used to read books that were at least 100 years old. I like it in principle, but find it difficult to practice it. At one time, I was a reading junkie.

This flair for reading changed, once I realized it was my time to 'give back' to the society by writing a few books. There is a *Principle of Conservation of Writing time and Reading time*. Anyway, here is an interesting story of a book. A month ago, I received a complimentary copy of *HULCHUL: THE COMMON INGREDIENT OF MOTION AND TIME* by Sohan Jain. Besides, common Indian math background, we have common friends of 40+ years. It was weird to notice that our parent publishing company is the same!

The Preface of the book hooked my interest, as it further connected us with Einstein's *Theory of Relativity* that I independently studied during 1961-62. I quit it for a number of reasons - however, Sohan continued and this book is inspired by the notion of *Time Dilation* in *Relativity*. He writes: "In the last four decades, not single day passed when I did not think at least for a few minutes, sometimes for hours, about time dilation in particular and time in general, and an intrinsic and deeper relationship between time and motion in the light of time dilation.........However, I enjoyed every moment of my research when it was frustrating and when it was productive."

Sohan quit on his Indian PhD, when an opportunity came along to immigrate to the US in 1960s. He did MS in computer science and recently retired as an IT executive. This book is a product of such a passionate pursuit of *time dilation* that he had filled out twelve composition notebooks. He never discussed and shared his work with anyone – a typical of a mathematician, and Hindu in particular.

Sohan typifies a Hindu mindset - pursuing knowledge for the sake of knowledge - all alone for years and independently. He earned my esteem for it and I decided to examine this book in right earnest. It is not filled with mathematical vocabulary of algebra, geometry and calculus. Instead, it has a lot of symbolism and notations never seen before. It is paramount to understand them very carefully.

Two weeks ago, we had a long discussion on his 'assumption' of *time dilation*. We all experience it psychologically, but where are mathematical equations to back it up? It does follow from Theory of Relativity that time slows down with high speeds comparable to the speed of light etc. Sohan seems to 'assume' it and claims on proving some results derived from Theory of Relativity. To some extent, mathematical rigor that lacked in Indian math curriculum through the 1950s is reflected in his writings.

I rushed on this book with the sort of feelings that are aroused on running into an old flame! I thought understanding of this work might lead to some future collaboration on *time dilation*. While feverishly working on my third book, I just could not go beyond the Introduction and the first five pages! It is not the first time that I felt stone walled by a subject matter.

It reminds me of a historic meeting, at Cambridge University, between George Polya (1887-1985), a great Hungarian mathematician and GH Hardy (1877- 1947), a doyen of English mathematicians. Hardy handed over to Polya some recent results of legendary Ramanujan (1887-1920), Hardy's research collaborator. Within minutes of perusing a sheaf of papers, he politely gave them back to Hardy with a famous line: "If I spent time in understanding Ramanujan's work, then I won't have time left to do my own researches."

That sums up my setting this book aside at age of 72 – no embarrassment in putting it away for a far more accomplishment to come out later this month. Of course, I would be going back to **HULCHUL** and periodically engage Sohan in conversations. *Time dilation* has several undertones - from poetic to philosophical to mathematical – all dear to me. In the meanwhile, I have suggested Sohan to start presenting these results in the regional mathematics meetings of the AMS and MAA.

May 31, 2012

COMMENTS

Time .....a fascinating concept not mathematically speaking I am poor in algebra, in fact, I get petrified and hence chose engg sciences where one get away with trigonometry and calculus which I am rather fond of . Kala....Time Krishna says He is Time' *na antam na madhyam napunastuvadam'* dimensionless quantity He says He is Time the Infinite...*'kalosmi lokaka kshaya pravriddhi......* I am Time that destroys and rebuilds over and over...he tells Arjun when asked who you are...a beautiful hyperbole from Vyas. Regs **Patro**

2. What an interesting guy you are -- with such varied interests! Regards, **Harbans**

3. Dear Satish, I hope you don't mind my addressing you as above. The more I talk with and read you, the more admiration I develop for you. This last (Truce with a book) letter of yours was a let down at first but not after reading till the last and looking at the title once again. It requires some courage to put down a book that you have begun to read with a lot of expectation.

I smiled a little at your reference to some people who read 100-year old books. This is because for the last few months I have been reading over 100 years old books. I can't buy recent books nor do I have friends here (in this essentially Gujarati city) who buy and read English books from whom I can borrow them. I am retired without a pension and have no regular income so cannot buy any inessential object, let alone books. So what do I do? Well, my son has been good enough to present me with an i-pad and I download free books and then read them. Most of the free downloadable books are those that were published in the 19th century so I have a great time reading the works of Charles Dickens, Jules Verne, Mark Twain, Lewis Carrol, H. Rider Haggard and so on.

Right from today, I have started reading a relatively new book The Man who knew infinity by Robert Kanigel. As you might know, it is a biography of Ramanujan. The copy has come to me because I have been told to translate it into Gujarati. There is an ambitious scheme in this 125th year of Ramanujan's birth to get Kanigel's book translated into all Indian languages.

So, keep 'm coming for us to read and enjoy! ..... **Arun Vaidya**

4. Hi Satish: I liked the way you shared your reason to not read the book, *Halchul*. Your reasons are the facts of life that you shared without hurting the person. **Alok**

A RELIGIOUS NUMBER -108

[**Introduction**: This is not my typical reflection, but is a modified write-up from a forwarded e-mail received a year or two ago. In each culture, there are numbers that are considered auspicious or inauspicious - like bad omens. However, it must be added that relatively speaking, numerology is very popular amongst the Hindu masses. How deep does it go mathematically is an open research problem in the area of ethno-mathematics.]

When we see the number of beads in *vara mala/vrata mala,* (terms for a rosary) the number of names of the God and Goddess, a question arises as to why so much importance is given to 108 in Hinduism? Why is 108 so sacred for the Hindus? There seems to be pattern of its presence in different scenarios listed below:

The diameter of the Sun is 108 times the diameter of the Earth. The distance from the Sun to the Earth is 108 times the diameter of the Sun. The average distance of the Moon from the Earth is 108 times the diameter of the Moon.

In *Ayurveda*, there are 108 *"marma"*, the points, which are vital for the living beings. The 'powerful' *Sri Chakra yantra* intersects in 54 points each with a masculine and feminine quality, totaling to 108. In Indian astrology, there are 12 houses and 9 planets. Thus, 12 times 9 equals to 108. In *Tantra*, (a form of Hath yoga), it is estimated that every day, we breathe 21,600 times out of which 10,800 belong to solar energy and 10, 800 are lunar energy – 10,800 = 108 x 100.

The saint Bharata wrote the famous, *Natya Shastra* (a treatise on the dances) which has 108 *karanas* (movements of hand and feet). There are 54 letters in Sanskrit language - each one can be mentioned as masculine (Shiva) and feminine (Shakti) aspect, totaling to 108. There are 108 *Puranas* and 108 *Upanishads*. 108 = 9 x 12. Both of these numbers are said to have spiritual and philosophical significance in many other Eastern traditions.

A mathematical symmetry is seen when 108 is written in the exponent form, $1^1 x 2^2 x 3^3$. Also, 108 is a Harshad number, which is an integer divisible by the sum of its digits (*Harshad* means, great joy in Hindi).

There are said to be 108 earthly **desires** in mortals and 108 **lies** that humans tell. There are said to be 108 human **delusions** or forms of ignorance. I see some fuzziness here. The *chakras* are the intersections of energy lines, and there are said to be a total of 108 energy lines converging to/from the heart chakra. One of them, *sushumna* leading to the crown chakra, which is said to be a path to self-realization.

If one is able to be so calm in meditation as to have only 108 breaths in a day, 'Enlightenment' will come. On the *Sri Yantra,* there are *marmas* where three lines intersect, and there are 54 such intersections. Each intersection has masculine and feminine, *shiva* and *shakti* qualities. 54 times 2 equal 108. Thus, there are 108 points that define the Sri Yantra as well as the human body.

It is said that there are 108 **feelings**, with 36 related to the past, 36 related to the present, and 36 related to the future. There are 12 constellations, and 9 arc segments called *namshas* or *chandrakalas.* 9 x12 = 108. *Chandra* is moon, and *kalas* are the divisions within a whole.

The sacred River Ganga spans a longitude of 12 degrees (79 to 91), and latitude of 9 degrees (22 to 31). There were said to be 108 *gopis* (divine consorts) of Krishna. According to some mythologists the digits 1, 0, and 8 in 108 means: 1 stands for God or higher Truth, 0 stands for emptiness or completeness in spiritual practice, and 8 stands for infinity or eternity. In astrology, the metal silver is said to represent the moon. The atomic weight of silver is 108.

There are 108 styles of meditation, and thus 108 paths to Godhood. In the Jain religion, 108 are the combined virtues of five categories of holy ones, including 12, 8, 36, 25, and 27 virtues respectively. The *mala* in Sikh tradition also has 108 knots tied in a string of wool, rather than beads. Some Buddhists carve 108 small Buddhas on a walnut for good luck. Some ring a bell 108 times to celebrate a new year. There are said to be 108 virtues to cultivate and 108 defilements to avoid. The Chinese Buddhists and Taoists use a 108-bead string, which is called *su-chu*, and has three dividing beads, so the mala is divided into three parts of 36 each.

According to the Chinese astrology, there are 108 sacred stars. It is said that **Atman**, the human soul goes through 108 stages on the journey. **Meru** is a larger bead, not part of the other 108 beads. It is not tied in the sequence of the other beads. It is the guiding bead, the one that marks the beginning and end of the mala. There are 108 qualities of praiseworthy souls. In **Japan**, at the end of the year, a bell is chimed 108 times to finish the old year and welcome the new one. Each ring represents one of 108 earthly temptations a person must overcome to achieve *nirvana.* The number 108 claims to signify the wholeness of the divinity and perfect totality.

June, 2012 – 2014

PERSONAL REMARKS

TIME TO 'COME OUT' AND RUN THE RACES!

A Reflective Narrative of Application for
The Barrick Distinguished Scholar Award

I. **Scholarly Work**: Let me place all my marbles down - my books published by Trafford:

1. *Scattered Matherticles, Mathematical Reflections, Volume I.* (Nov, 2010)

2. *Vectors in History: Main Foci; India and USA, Volume I.* (Jan, 2012)

3. *Epsilons and Deltas of Life: Everyday Stories, Volume I.* (June, 2012)

4. *My Hindu Faith and Periscope, Volume I.* (Nov, 2012)

5. *Via Bathinda: Reflective Memoirs, Volume I* (To be released in Feb, 2013)

In Pipeline: Nearly a dozen – God willing (*Insha'Allah!*)

Contents: The body of my work may be categorized as non-fiction reflective genre. The contents of the first book are **mathematical** in nature – but, no hard-core mathematics is included. In textbook writing, it is challenging to be original - say, in the area of calculus, all textbooks are isomorphic. The second book has **historical** *Reflections* – pure history. However, a separate volume on *History of Mathematics* is planned for Spring-2014. The third book has **philosophical** *Reflections* – but free from philosophical jargon. The fourth book has **religious** *Reflections*. It comes out of a thesis that an organized religion eventually seeps into the foundations of every activity of its follower. Hinduism is my faith.

II. **Background**: Since the inception of Barrick Scholar Awards, 30 years ago, I never thought of applying for one. Michael Golberg (1941- 2008 & Distinguished Nevadan-2012) was the first math faculty recipient. My two mathematical reflections, ***Michael Golberg: a pure researcher*** (p 164-165) and ***An Euler I Know*** (p 168-170) are included in Book # 1 listed above. The point is that Michael set a benchmark on a track that I was not even running on!

Early History: When I joined UNLV in 1974, it had no PhD program; only half the faculty had math PhDs. It must be added that in the worst unemployment conditions in the 1970s, caused by the Middle East oil embargo, I did not apply to even a single PhD granting institution. Prior to coming to the US, because of my seven years of college teaching in India, my professional goal has been to achieve excellence in every aspect of teaching and related scholarly activities.

During the first year, I enthusiastically taught **eight different courses** in the areas of pure math, applied math and computer science. Moreover, the courses were spread out - from remedial to senior/graduate levels. In order to put it in perspective, lately, math faculty coming up for promotion and tenure, end up teaching not more than **six different courses** during their **first six years** at UNLV! Currently, in the first academic year, the teaching load of the new hires is 1-1, which rises to 1-2 for the next two years, and then stays 2-2 generally.

Bifurcation: The Nomination Requirements for Barrick Scholar Awards include "....*candidate's research program or creative accomplishments is required...*", while, for many years, my research and scholarly activities were amorphous. Because of my passion for teaching, my traditional research in mathematics was minimal at the time of each promotion and tenure. It was after three unsuccessful applications that promotion to (full) professorship came to me in 1990. Not even once, did I file a grievance. Reason: call it my Hindu upbringing!

However, each personnel 'set back' made me steadier and strong believer in my pathless path of scholarly activities. Numerous Chautauqua courses that I continue to attend (22) and regular papers that are presented (32) in the areas of History of Mathematics, Mathematics Education, and Philosophy of Mathematics keep me oxygenated. Some of them are included in my books.

My Intellectual involution and evolution: The enormity of my writings, done over the years, is quite a pile. I had no idea how each *Reflection* would stand up. The growing pile started looking like a galaxy that gives a structure to the individual stars in the firmament. It was never showcased. Again, it comes from a culture I grew up in India and Hindu faith that raised me: "Always, be humble, be obedient, don't show off, walk with your gaze down, etc." It sums up the building blocks of my life in India through the 1960s. It took me decades to realize that political freedom of a nation is one thing, but for its individuals to have a free mind is quite different. I thank the US for this inner transformation.

Impact of my work: Through teaching, I can claim to have touched a few lives. It is reflected in an all-time record of having taught 52 different catalog courses, and designed and taught 15 experimental courses and honors seminars. *Charming Transfinite Numbers*, *Mathematical Thinking in Liberal Arts* and *Paradoxes in Arts, Science and Mathematics* are my all-time innovative offerings. This diversity in teaching is directly proportional to the diversity of themes of my books. My teaching and scholarly activities have actually submerged into one stream.

The first proof of impact of a literary work lies in a noticeable change in the author's intellectual development. In a mathematical parlance, it is recursive. A piece of creative work emanating from a mind, after a period of gestation, impinges on it again under different conditions. It gives me a new high and surreal feelings whenever I read, edit and compile the 'old' *Reflections*.

Presently, I am so engrossed in writing that I have no idea how my books have been influencing the readers. At least 2-3 persons have been 'inspired' to take up on creative writing. Over the last 12 years, a couple of hundred friends and relatives, and their friends and relatives have embarked upon on a mind journey with me. Their lives are touched, as some of their comments are included in each volume - except for the first one. Book reviews, posted on Amazon, do measure some impact. Recently, I Googled my name and was astonished to see 20 pages bearing it. It is despite the fact that I do not have any website, blog, Tweet or Facebook etc.

To my Hindu friends, I tell that the goddess ***Saraswati*** (of knowledge) and ***Durga*** (of valor) are sitting on my shoulders, as I am able to think at a level that I had hitherto never dreamed. How long their blessings will remain, I have no idea. Therefore, I want to mine out as many nuggets as possible, and as quickly as possible. To my other friends, I tell that most professors are considered dead wood after the age of 60, and here, I wrote my first book at the age of 71. Two years ago, I captured this experience with that of a man who fathers a child at 70 - of course, without any shots of Viagra and testosterones!

Future Work: Yes, there will be at least a second volume for each of the five books listed above; the first book will go for the third one. Having spent over 50 years in collegiate education, not writing a volume on education would sound incongruous. Also, for a year, I was the Associate Chair of the Department, and for three years, Associate Dean of the College. Those positions have given me perspectives on higher education that a faculty member, in general, has no ideas. The material for one volume is ready. It is not out of place to point out that in the 55-year history of UNLV, only six other math faculty members have written books – all textbooks and research monographs, which largely include the published research papers.

Unabashedly, I state that my books are unique in ideas, formats, layouts, and even the covers – all are products of my imagination. On being repeatedly queried, how do I do it? Here is an answer that eventually surfaced up my mind. Mathematics is not just a formidable discipline; it is also a powerful tool, as real as a universal wrench in a garage. Furthermore, it is a language - not just of the sciences since the times of Galileo, but now of all disciplines - including fine arts and humanities!

Above all, the 'nuclear power' of mathematics lies in its deductive reasoning - the essence of mathematical thinking. However, the power of deductive thinking in diverse areas can only be unleashed from the minds of the unshackled mathematicians. It is very difficult for a traditional mathematician to de-condition his/her mind, and then divert its energy in other disciplines. In modern times, to the best of my knowledge, Bertrand Russell (1872-1970) is the only mathematician who has done it under the most bizarre circumstances. Subsequently, he made new histories in literature (Nobel Laureate, 1950), politics of pacifism (nominated for the Noble Peace Prize), education, and social issues.

Finally, the converse of the above 'theorem' is not true!

Nov 16, 2012/March, 2015

PS: 03/01/2015

I was not the winner in 2012 and 2013, and declined to apply in 2014.

COMMENTS

Dear Satish, Great Record! You deserve to be proud of yourself. We are, of course, proud of you. As a writer's Revenge, I am imposing on you my own most recent paper --will see if you are as good a reader as you are a writer! **Harbans Singh Bhola**

2. My dear Satish, I am simply amazed at your intellectual output for the benefit of humanity. My warmest congratulations and greetings to you and to that great woman behind you, your dear wife that made it happen. With my best wishes and hoping to see you soon in India, sincerely, **S.R. Wadhwa**

3. There is no doubt your own life (intellectually and otherwise) has been enriched by your dedication to writing. By writing, any of us can become a better and more lucid thinker. Also, I believe when any of us enjoy something so much as you enjoy writing, we can live longer and healthier lives.

Many of your friends (me included) have enjoyed a majority of your pieces. As you know, I have strong disagreements with you on some issues and some of your paradigms of thinking and framing history. But like me, you are entitled to your opinions. Congratulations, Satish! Write on! **Amritjit Singh**

I wrote: In the world of mathematics, if two persons disagree on the proof of a statement, then one is certainly wrong. However, in the world, complement of mathematics, if two thinkers agree all the time, then one is not thinking at all!

4.   You are great! **Prem Singh**

5.   Hi Satish: Your professional account captures your intellectual pursuits and the rationale behind your creative work and your engaging active mind. Good luck with your application for Barrick Distinguished Scholar Award application. Surely, you deserve recognition. **Moorty**

6.   Satish, I wish you success in your application. Your intellectual interests are so diverse. **Noel Pugach**

7.   An impressive résumé...**Neal Smatresk**

8.   Satish, Thank you for this. I appreciate both the wisdom and wit (Viagra and testosterone) in this reflection. Many thanks for sharing with me and sincere wishes of good luck in your pursuit of this award. Best wishes, **Richard Schori**

COMMENTATORS & ANALYSTS EXTRAORDINAIRE

Fourteen years ago, I started writing **Reflections,** a reincarnation of my life-long passion of writing all kinds of letters. The big difference was that that my reflective writings went public – from one to many, as I started sharing them with friends and relatives. And, from there, it went to their friends and relatives, and so on. Years ago, a student of mine created a blog, but seldom had I posted anything. I don't have a website either. It is all emails in a bcc - electronically old-fashioned mode.

I have several mailing lists and I am used to this inefficient mode of communication. I have Facebook and Twitter accounts too, but they too have remained unused. That is my approach to communication. Naturally, some of my readers write back and give comments. At times, a small dialog takes place. It has added clarity, expanded the topic, and sharpened my intellect – must at this stage of life.

For a number of reasons, not all the comments and commentators are included in the book– only those comments, which are concise and strong. In reflective style of writings, inclusion of comments adds a new flavor. Initially, I never saved the comments. Also, sometimes, no comments were received. That is why the spaces following some **Reflections** are blank.

It is not merely a time to thank them, but also share a piece of 'immortality' that this book may bring! When I look at the credentials of these persons, I am myself awed and wowed. These comments have come out of their incredible rich backgrounds. I don't think any other author can easily match this list. Here are the names in some order:

Raju Abraham, 65: Known for nine years. English professor – has taught in Baroda/India, Sana/Yemen, and presently in Oman with University of Nizwa, where I was a visiting professor during Spring-2009.

Francis Andrew, 65 is professor of English in the College of Applied Sciences, in Nizwa. His knowledge of Christian theology, astronomy and science in general is very extensive. He uses them effectively in writing science fiction books – nearly dozen. We met in 2009 and have been in regular touch since then.

Anand R. Bhatia, aged 71, is a retired professor of business from California State University, San Bernardino. We have known each other for 30+ years mainly for our common ideas and values, though we grew up extremes cities – he, in Mumbai and me, in Bathinda. Anand is a very good storywriter, but this flair is sacrificed for the time being for his love for real estate investments. I often tease him about marketing his voice and laughter, which are very deep and full.

Avnish Bhatnagar: My son, age 47, working at Google since 2006. His comments are fewer, but deep.

Rahul Bhatnagar, 55: Distantly related - physician by training in India. He has an interesting job of medical director of drug safety with a pharmaceutical company; very astute commentator and analyst of nearly all my *Reflections*. He can refine and dissect an issue to a state that becomes undistinguishable from the one started with.

Harbans Singh Bhola, 85: Emeritus professor of education, Indiana University, known since 1971. He had his bachelors with A and B courses that I had too. He has sharp intellect and a robust Punjabi sense of humor.

Larry Curnutt, age 70 and I joined IU for PhD at the same time in the fall of 1968. Larry left IU after five years without PhD, as his dissertation was not getting on a track. He then joined a 2-year college community college and spent all his life there - being fully at peace with academic life. I often tell graduate students that for pursuing a doctorate degree, the right choice of supervisor is the single most important gradient in the PhD mix!

Irma Dutchie is our next-door neighbor, that I call her, our angel now after 12 years. Both physically and mentally, she can challenge any 60-year old. She has a Bostonian aura about her life style. Her love for life is as phenomenal as helping friends, strangers and charity organizations with her time, money and energy. She is my inspiration for life. At 84, she says that she can't be without a boyfriend!

Robert P. Gilbert (83) my PhD advisor, and I was his last doctoral student before he left IU in 1974 for the University of Delaware via Germany for a year.

Germany. Late on, he joined University of Delaware as Unidel Chair professor and retired at the age of 80. However, he remains active in supervising doctoral students researching in mathematical biology. We have remained in contact ever since. Many times, he tried to pull me into his old and new researches, but I am following my drummer within. His love for math has not affected his love for many other pursuits in life – that is inspiring.

Aaron Harris, 35 was the best student in both the graduate courses that he took from me during 2006-07. He is about to get his PhD in Mathematics Education from UNLV - while teaching mathematics full time in a high school and raising four kids with his wife of fourteen years.

Robert Meyer, 50+ years old was my student in several courses Bob as an undergraduate and graduate student. He suffered from a stroke in his 20s, later hit by a car in his wheel chair. He won the Governor's award for getting over the handicaps. He retired as a computer programmer from the Air Force. He loves to tutor math. He is an acclaimed poet of Nevada, and his poetry reminds me John Milton.

Owen Nelson, 82 year old, has been a part time instructor at UNLV for over 15 years – hired for the sole purpose of teaching remedial math courses. He got his MS in science education from UW- Madison and ABD (All But Dissertation) from Indiana University. Owen is one of the rare individuals whose intellectual growth has not been limited by formal college degrees. He has extensively commented on most of my mathematical reflections. In a way, he has lived through historical events on many fronts. Often, his feedback brings out clarity in my thoughts. Owen stands out in contrast with many PhDs who seldom see, smell, talk or think out of a box of their narrow specializations.

IBS Passi, 76 years old is working as an honorary professor of mathematics in IISER while continuing to do his research in algebra. He was a senior to me during our maser's from PU Chandigarh, and has the unique distinction of topping the examinations both for his BA and MA. After PhD from UK, he taught at KU before moving to PU Chandigarh. We have been directly and indirectly in touch with each other ever since. He is a member of Indian Academy of Science, and has served as President of the IMS.

Subhash C. Saxena, 78: known for 20-30 years – all due to our common participation in th national and international math meetings. For the last four years he has been promoting his book on Collegr Geometry at every conference. A few years ago, he took retirement from Coastal University in North Carolina.

BhuDev Sharma 77: Known since 1990, math professor - taught in India, Trinidad and several universities in the US. He organized World Association of Vedic Studies and its biennial conferences in India and the USA. He is an able educational administrator. For several years, published the *Vishwa Vivek*, the first Hindi monthly magazine in the US.

Ved P. Sharma, 76: friends since 1964 when we taught in Panjab University, Shimla. Twelve years of chairing the Department of Economics in Mankato State took a toll on his back and knees. He is now working fulltime one semester at a time.

Looy Simonoff: retired from UNLV in 2000. He is the only colleague who also remained a family friend until his death in 2011 - at the age of 83. Teaching mathematical rigor in every course was somewhat religious with him – no matter how unpopular he was in students' evaluation of his courses.

Harpreet Singh, 40: A rare combination of computer science, finance, active spirituality, and creative writing – always exploring and stretching his limits. He is 39 years old and known for 15 years – initially through his parents.

Sarvajit Singh, 75 and I have been known to each other since 1965 at KU. He is an established researcher in mathematical seismology and author. After years at KU, he moved to MDU Rohtak where he serves and Professor & Head of Math Dept. and Dean before retiring from there – but settled in Delhi. He is a member Indian National Academy of Sciences, and has also served as President of the IMS.

Subhash Sood: Physician by training in India, UK and USA - studied other systems of medicine too. He was deep into by Scientology and established a center in Ambala Cantt, and translated several scientology books from English into Hindi. He suddenly died of a stroke in 2007 at the age of 73 - in a 100-year old dilapidated mansion in which he was born. He was my most avid reader and friend for over 25 years.

E. Sooriamurthy, 76: Retired physics professor, Madurai University, India – known since 1968 – during our common PhD days at Indiana University, Bloomington. His son, Raja, computer science professor at Carnegie Mellon. They are second father-son duo and fan of my *Reflections*!

Shankar and Sangeetha Venkatagiri is a couple in their late 40s, who left their fulltime US jobs 15 years ago in order to settle back in India. I have come to know them through my son. Shankar got PhD in math from Georgia Tech, but now works for the IIM, Bangalore. Sangeetha is active in social work. They are the only US returned couple, personally known, who are now fully adjusted in India.

Arun Vaidya, 76: Retired professor and Head of Mathematics Department of Gujarat University. His uncle was also a well-known mathematician. We have been in communication for the last three years - since we met in a history of mathematics conference in Gujarat.

Len Zane, 70: Retired UNLV physics professor, who also served as the founding Director/Dean of the Honors College for ten years. We often chat and exchange ideas.